Current
CONTROVERSIES

The Arms Trade

Other Books in the Current Controversies Series

The Arms Trade

Noël Merino, Book Editor

GREENHAVEN PRESS
A part of Gale, Cengage Learning

GALE
CENGAGE Learning™

Detroit • New York • San Francisco • New Haven, Conn • Waterville, Maine • London

Christine Nasso, *Publisher*
Elizabeth Des Chenes, *Managing Editor*

© 2009 Greenhaven Press, a part of Gale, Cengage Learning

Gale and Greenhaven Press are registered trademarks used herein under license.

For more information, contact:
Greenhaven Press
27500 Drake Rd.
Farmington Hills, MI 48331-3535
Or you can visit our Internet site at gale.cengage.com

Articles in Greenhaven Press anthologies are often edited for length to meet page requirements. In addition, original titles of these works are changed to clearly present the main thesis and to explicitly indicate the author's opinion. Every effort is made to ensure that Greenhaven Press accurately reflects the original intent of the authors. Every effort has been made to trace the owners of copyrighted material.

Cover image © Daniel Hunger/dpa/Corbis.

LIBRARY OF CONGRESS CATALOGING-IN-PUBLICATION DATA

The arms trade / Noël Merino, book editor.
p. cm. -- (Current controversies)
Includes bibliographical references and index.
ISBN-13: 978-0-7377-4318-0 (hardcover)
ISBN-13: 978-0-7377-4317-3 (pbk.)
1. Defense industries. 2. Arms transfers. I. Merino, Noël.
HD9743.A2A746 2009
382'.456234--dc22

2008049211

Printed in the United States of America
1 2 3 4 5 6 7 13 12 11 10 09

Contents

Chapter 1: What Is the Current Status of the Arms Trade?

Chapter 2: Does the Arms Trade Increase Security?

Chapter 3: Does the Arms Trade Need More Global Regulation?

No: The Arms Trade Does Not Need More Global Regulation

Chapter 4: What Are Some of the Concerns About the Arms Trade?

Foreword

By definition, controversies are "discussions of questions in which opposing opinions clash" (*Webster's Twentieth Century Dictionary Unabridged*). Few would deny that controversies are a pervasive part of the human condition and exist on virtually every level of human enterprise. Controversies transpire between individuals and among groups, within nations and between nations. Controversies supply the grist necessary for progress by providing challenges and challengers to the status quo. They also create atmospheres where strife and warfare can flourish. A world without controversies would be a peaceful world; but it also would be, by and large, static and prosaic.

The Series' Purpose

The purpose of the Current Controversies series is to explore many of the social, political, and economic controversies dominating the national and international scenes today. Titles selected for inclusion in the series are highly focused and specific. For example, from the larger category of criminal justice, Current Controversies deals with specific topics such as police brutality, gun control, white collar crime, and others. The debates in Current Controversies also are presented in a useful, timeless fashion. Articles and book excerpts included in each title are selected if they contribute valuable, long-range ideas to the overall debate. And wherever possible, current information is enhanced with historical documents and other relevant materials. Thus, while individual titles are current in focus, every effort is made to ensure that they will not become quickly outdated. Books in the Current Controversies series will remain important resources for librarians, teachers, and students for many years.

In addition to keeping the titles focused and specific, great care is taken in the editorial format of each book in the series. Book introductions and chapter prefaces are offered to provide background material for readers. Chapters are organized around several key questions that are answered with diverse opinions representing all points on the political spectrum. Materials in each chapter include opinions in which authors clearly disagree as well as alternative opinions in which authors may agree on a broader issue but disagree on the possible solutions. In this way, the content of each volume in Current Controversies mirrors the mosaic of opinions encountered in society. Readers will quickly realize that there are many viable answers to these complex issues. By questioning each author's conclusions, students and casual readers can begin to develop the critical thinking skills so important to evaluating opinionated material.

Current Controversies is also ideal for controlled research. Each anthology in the series is composed of primary sources taken from a wide gamut of informational categories including periodicals, newspapers, books, U.S. and foreign government documents, and the publications of private and public organizations. Readers will find factual support for reports, debates, and research papers covering all areas of important issues. In addition, an annotated table of contents, an index, a book and periodical bibliography, and a list of organizations to contact are included in each book to expedite further research.

Perhaps more than ever before in history, people are confronted with diverse and contradictory information. During the Persian Gulf War, for example, the public was not only treated to minute-to-minute coverage of the war, it was also inundated with critiques of the coverage and countless analyses of the factors motivating U.S. involvement. Being able to sort through the plethora of opinions accompanying today's major issues, and to draw one's own conclusions, can be a complicated and frustrating struggle. It is the editors' hope that Current Controversies will help readers with this struggle.

Introduction

"The initial arms-importing country is not necessarily the final destination for the weapons or technology."

The arms trade is part of the arms industry, a thriving global business that includes the manufacturing and selling of weapons and military technology. World military expenditures in 2006 are estimated to be more than one trillion dollars.[1] Though much of this military money is spent domestically on arms, training, and intelligence, over $40 billion of the total is spent in the international arms arena.[2] Since 1950, the United States, Russia, Germany, France, and the United Kingdom have been the five main global arms exporters. Topping the list of importers are China, India, Greece, and the United Arab Emirates. The initial arms-importing country is not necessarily the final destination for the weapons or technology. Often the goods are resold to nations or rogue regimes that are unable to openly purchase weapons and technology in the arms market. For example, during the month-long war between Israel and Hezbollah in southern Lebanon in the summer of 2006, Hezbollah used arms it had obtained from outsiders, such as Iran and Syria.

Hezbollah is a Shiite Islamic paramilitary organization in Lebanon, which has had a significant impact on Lebanon's politics. Founded in 1982, in response to the Israeli invasion of Lebanon, it has close ties to Iran and Syria. One of Hezbollah's primary stated goals is the elimination of the state of Israel, and it has advocated for the establishment of an Iranian-style Islamic government in Lebanon. Because of the United States' ongoing support for Israel, Hezbollah has frequently attacked America and its Western allies in its war against Israel. Hezbollah has been linked to kidnappings of

Westerners in Lebanon in the 1980s, a 1983 suicide truck bombing at a U.S. Marines barracks in Beirut, and the hijacking of TWA Flight 847. The United States, Israel, the Netherlands, and Canada consider Hezbollah a terrorist organization, though within much of Lebanon and the Muslim world it is regarded as a legitimate political organization.

After the 2006 war between Israel and Lebanon, the United Nations imposed a ban on arms sales to Hezbollah. The United Nation's Security Council Resolution 1701 also called for a permanent ceasefire between Israel and Lebanon, as well as complete disarmament of Hezbollah. Many of the weapons Hezbollah used during the war, such as automatic rifles, rocket-propelled grenades, mortars, and Katyusha rockets, as well as cruise missiles, tanks, and armored carriers, came from Iran and Syria, as previously noted. But originally, at least some of the arms came from China, via Iran, and from Russia, via Syria. Iran and Syria have been implicated in arming Hezbollah since the war, despite the embargo, but the two countries deny this.

Israel has applied pressure to world leaders to prevent arms smuggling to Hezbollah in Lebanon through Syria, and international diplomats have warned Syria about this matter. A Shiite member of parliament in Lebanon confirmed that, two years later, Hezbollah has more arms than during the 2006 war with Israel—approximately 27,000 rockets and missiles, according to Israeli officials.[3] Though Hezbollah has accumulated numerous weapons, thus threatening the stability of Lebanon, the Lebanese national unity government issued a statement in August of 2008 proclaiming that the organization can keep its weapons.

The conflict between Lebanon, with the armed paramilitary organization Hezbollah, and Israel illustrates many of the issues surrounding the arms trade debate: the problem with illicit arms trading, the concern about the ultimate destination of legally traded arms, and the absence of globally binding

17

controls. Arms are, at times, traded in full public view and, at other times, smuggled without detection. There are no mandatory global controls on the arms trade and United Nations embargoes are often ignored. By presenting different views on the status of the arms trade worldwide, the justifications for this trade, possible arms trade controls, and other concerns, *Current Controversies: The Arms Trade* sheds light on this widespread trade of potentially deadly goods.

Notes

1. *SIPRI Yearbook 2007: Armaments, Disarmament, and International Security.* Oxford University Press, 2007.

2. Thom Shanker, "U.S. Leads Arms Sales to Developing Countries," *International Herald Tribune*, September 30, 2007.

3. "Hezbollah Has More Arms, Personnel than 2006," Agence France-Presse, August 8, 2008.

CHAPTER 1

What Is the Current Status of the Arms Trade?

The Global Arms Trade: An Overview

Richard F. Grimmett

Richard F. Grimmett is a specialist in national defense with the Foreign Affairs, Defense, and Trade Division of the Congressional Research Service (CRS), the public policy research arm of the U.S. Congress.

The value of all arms transfer agreements worldwide (to both developed and developing nations) in 2006 was $40.3 billion. This was a decrease in arms agreements values over 2005, a decline of nearly 13%.

Arms Transfer Agreements Worldwide

In 2006, the United States led in arms transfer *agreements worldwide*, making agreements valued at $16.9 billion (41.9% of all such agreements) up from $13.5 billion in 2005. Russia ranked second with $8.7 billion in agreements (21.6% of these agreements globally), up from $7.5 billion in 2005. The United Kingdom ranked third, its arms transfer agreements worldwide standing at $3.1 billion in 2006, up from $2.9 billion in 2005. The United States, Russia, and the United Kingdom collectively made agreements in 2006 valued at $28.7 billion, 71.2% of all international arms transfer agreements made by all suppliers.

For the period 2003–2006, the total value of all international arms transfer agreements ($160 billion) was higher than the worldwide value during 1999–2002 ($156.7 billion), an increase of 2.1%. During the period 1999–2002, developing world nations accounted for 67.1% of the value of all arms transfer agreements made worldwide. During 2003–2006, de-

Richard F. Grimmett, *Conventional Arms Transfers to Developing Nations, 1999–2006*, Congressional Research Service (CRS) Report for Congress, September 26, 2007, pp. 4–8. http://www.fas.org/sgp/crs/weapons/RL34187.pdf.

veloping world nations accounted for 65.7% of all arms transfer agreements made globally. In 2006, developing nations accounted for 71.5% of all arms transfer agreements made worldwide.

Arms Deliveries Worldwide

In 2006, the United States ranked first in the value of all arms *deliveries worldwide*, making $14 billion in such deliveries or 51.9%. This is the eighth year in a row that the United States has led in global arms deliveries. Russia ranked second in worldwide arms deliveries in 2006, making $5.8 billion in such deliveries. The United Kingdom ranked third in 2006, making $3.3 billion in such deliveries. These top three suppliers of arms in 2006 collectively delivered nearly $23.1 billion, 85.6% of all arms delivered worldwide by all suppliers in that year.

Worldwide weapons orders declined in 2006.

The value of all international arms deliveries in 2006 was $27 billion. This is an increase in the total value of arms deliveries from the previous year (a rise from $26.2 billion), but still the second lowest deliveries total for the 1999–2006 period. Moreover, the total value of such arms deliveries worldwide in 2003–2006 ($120.7 billion) was substantially lower in the value of arms deliveries by all suppliers worldwide from 1999–2002 ($144.8 billion, a decline of over $24 billion).

Developing nations from 2003–2006 accounted for 73.3% of the value of all international arms deliveries. In the earlier period, 1999–2002, developing nations accounted for 71.7% of the value of all arms deliveries worldwide. In 2006, developing nations collectively accounted for 73.6% of the value of all international arms deliveries.

Arms Orders Worldwide

Worldwide weapons orders declined in 2006. The total of $40.3 billion, fell from $46.3 billion in 2005, a decline of nearly 13%. Global arms agreement values for the years other than 2006 ranged from $46.3 billion in 2005 to $31.7 billion in 2003. Of the major arms orders secured in 2006 most were made by the traditional major suppliers. In some instances these orders represented significant new acquisitions by the purchasing country. In others they reflected the continuation of a longer term weapons acquisition program.

The United States and European countries . . . seem likely to compete vigorously for prospective arms contracts within the European region in the foreseeable future.

A decline in new weapons sales can also be explained, in part, by the practical need for some purchasing nations to absorb and integrate major weapons systems they have already purchased into their force structures. The need to do this may, at the same time, increase the number of arms contracts related to training and support services, even as it reduces the number of large and costly orders for new military equipment.

Competition in the Arms Market

An intensely competitive weapons marketplace continues to lead several producing countries to focus sales efforts on prospective clients in nations and regions where individual suppliers have had competitive advantages resulting from well established military support relationships. Within Europe, arms sales to new NATO [North Atlantic Treaty Organization] member nations to support their military modernization programs have created new business for arms suppliers, while allowing these NATO states to sell some of their older generation military equipment, in refurbished form, to other less-developed countries. While there are inherent limitations on these European sales due to the smaller defense budgets of many of the purchasing countries, creative seller financing options, as well as the use of co-assembly, co-production, and counter-trade agreements to offset costs to the buyers, have continued to facilitate new arms agreements. The United States and European countries or consortia seem likely to compete vigorously for prospective arms contracts within the European region in the foreseeable future. Such sales seem particularly important to European suppliers, as they can potentially compensate, in part, for lost weapons deals elsewhere in the developing world that result from reduced demand for new weapons.

Efforts also continue among developed nations to protect important elements of their national military industrial bases by limiting arms purchases from other developed nations. Nevertheless, several key arms suppliers have placed additional emphasis on joint production of various weapons systems with other developed nations as a more effective way to preserve a domestic weapons production capability, while sharing the costs of new weapons development. The consolidation of certain sectors of the domestic defense industries of key weapons producing nations continues, in the face of intense foreign competition. At the same time, some supplying nations have chosen to manufacture items for niche weapons categories where their specialized production capabilities give them important advantages in the evolving international arms marketplace.

The Purchases of Developing Nations

Some developing nations have reduced their weapons purchases in recent years primarily due to their limited financial resources to pay for such equipment. Other prospective arms purchasers in the developing world with significant financial assets have exercised caution in launching new and costly weapons procurement programs. Increases in the price of oil, while an advantage for major oil producing states in funding their arms purchases, has, simultaneously, caused economic difficulties for many oil consuming states, contributing to their decisions to defer or curtail new weapons purchases. The state of the world economy has induced a number of developing nations to choose to upgrade existing weapons systems in their inventories, while reducing their purchases of new ones. This approach may curtail sales of new weapons systems for a time, but the weapons upgrade market can be very lucrative for some arms producers, and partially mitigate the effect of losing major new sales.

Although, overall, there appear to be fewer large weapons purchases being made by developing nations in the Near East and in Asia, when contrasted with arms sales activity over a decade ago, major purchases continue to be made by a select few developing nations in these regions. These purchases have been made principally by China and India in Asia, and Saudi Arabia in the Near East. Even though these tendencies are subject to abrupt change based on the strength of either the regional or international economies, or the threat assessments of individual states, the strength of individual economies of a wide range of nations in the developing world continues to be a significant factor in the timing of many of their arms purchasing decisions.

Recently, from 2003–2006, the United States and Russia have dominated the arms market in the developing world.

Latin America, and, to a much lesser extent, Africa, are regions where some nations continue to express interest in modernizing important sectors of their military forces. Some large arms orders (by regional standards) have been placed by a few states in these two regions within the last decade. But in Latin America and Africa, as with most nations in the developing world, nations are constrained in their weapons purchases by their existing financial resources. So long as there is limited availability of seller-supplied credit and financing for weapons purchases, and national budgets for military purchases remain relatively low, it seems likely that major arms sales to these two regions of the developing world will remain sporadic in nature.

Arms Transfer Agreements with Developing Nations

The value of all arms transfer *agreements* with developing nations in 2006 was nearly $28.8 billion, a decrease from the $31.8 billion total in 2005. In 2006, the value of all arms *deliveries* to developing nations ($19.9 billion) was lower than the value of 2005 deliveries (over $20.3 billion), and the lowest total for the 1999–2006 period.

The U.S. appears likely to hold its position as the principal supplier to key developing world nations.

Recently, from 2003–2006, the United States and Russia have dominated the arms market in the developing world. The United States ranked first for 3 out of 4 years during this period, while Russia ranked second for 3 out of 4 of these years in the value of arms transfer *agreements*. From 2003–2006, the United States made $34.1 billion in arms transfer agreements with developing nations, 32.4% of all such agreements. Russia, the second leading supplier during this period, made $25.8 billion in arms transfer agreements or 24.5%. The United Kingdom, the third leading supplier, from 2003–2006 made $10.5 billion or 10% of all such agreements with developing nations during these years. In the earlier period (1999–2002) the United States ranked first with $45.4 billion in arms transfer agreements with developing nations or 43.1%; Russia made $25.4 billion in arms transfer agreements during this period or 24.1%. France made $5.5 billion in agreements or 5.2%.

The Major Suppliers of Arms to Developing Nations

From 1999–2006, most arms transfers to developing nations were made by two to three major suppliers in any given year. The United States has ranked first among these suppliers for seven of the last eight years during this period, falling to third place in 2005. Russia has been a continuing strong competitor for the lead in arms transfer agreements with developing nations, ranking second every year from 1999 through 2004, and first in 2005. Despite its lack of the larger traditional client base for armaments held by the United States and the major West European suppliers, Russia's recent successes in concluding new arms orders suggests that Russia is likely to continue to be, for the short term at least, a significant leader in arms agreements with developing nations. Russia's most significant high value arms transfer agreements continue to be with China and India, Russia has had some success in concluding arms agreements with clients beyond its principal two. Russia continues to seek to expand its prospects in North Africa, the Middle East, and Southeast Asia.

The wealthier developing countries continue as the focus for new arms sales by the principal supplying nations.

Most recently Russia has increased sales efforts in Latin America, despite having essentially abandoned major arms sales efforts there following the Cold War's end. Venezuela has become a significant new arms client gained by Russia in this region. The Russian government has further stated that it has adopted more flexible payment arrangements for its prospective customers in the developing world, including a willingness in specific cases to forgive outstanding debts owed to it by a prospective client in order to secure new arms purchases. Furthermore, Russia continues its efforts to enhance the quality of its follow-on support services to make Russian products more attractive and competitive, and to assure its potential clients that it can effectively provide timely service for weapons systems it exports.

Major West European arms suppliers, such as France and the United Kingdom, have concluded large orders with developing countries over the last eight years, based on either long-term supply relationships or their having specialized weapons systems they can readily provide. Germany has been a key source of naval systems for developing nations. Despite increased competition between the United States and the other major arms suppliers, the U.S. appears likely to hold its position as the principal supplier to key developing world nations, especially those able to afford major new weapons. Because the United States has developed such a wide base of arms equipment clients globally it is able to conclude a notable number of agreements annually to provide upgrades, ordnance and support services for the large variety of weapons systems it has sold to its clients for decades. Thus, even when the U.S. does not conclude major new arms agreements in a given year, it can still register significant arms agreement values based on transactions in these other categories.

The wealthier developing countries continue as the focus for new arms sales by the principal supplying nations. Arms transfers to the less affluent developing nations also continue to be constrained by the scarcity of funds in their defense budgets, and the unsettled state of the international economy. The overall decline in the level of the arms agreements with developing nations that began in 2001 and continued until 2004, appears to have halted. There was a rise in arms agreements with the developing world in 2004 and again in 2005. Although there was a decline in arms agreements with the developing world in 2006, the overall level of arms agreements with such nations from 2004–2006 has been on the increase.

Non-Major Arms Suppliers to Developing Nations

China, other European, and non-European suppliers, such as Sweden and Israel, appear to have increased their participation in the arms trade with the developing world in recent years, albeit at a much lower level, and with uneven results, than those of the major suppliers. Nevertheless, these non-major arms suppliers have proven capable, on occasion, of making arms deals of consequence. Most of their annual arms transfer agreement values during 1999–2006 have been comparatively low, although larger when they are aggregated together as a group. In various cases they have been successful in selling older generation equipment, even while they procure newer weaponry to update their own military forces. These arms suppliers also are more likely to be sources of small arms and light weapons, and associated ordnance, rather than routine sellers of major military equipment. Most of these arms suppliers are not likely to consistently rank with the traditional major suppliers of advanced weaponry in the value of their arms agreements and deliveries.

Information on the Small Arms Trade Is Incomplete

Jeff Abramson

Jeff Abramson is the managing editor of Arms Control Today, *a magazine published by the Arms Control Association providing information, analysis, and commentary on arms control proposals, negotiations and agreements, and related national security issues.*

The number of countries voluntarily providing data to the United Nations [UN] on their small arms and light weapons trade has jumped substantially this year, shedding new light on the pervasiveness and complexity of this often murky commerce.

The UN Register of Conventional Arms

As of early October [2007], 30 states had declared their small arms and light weapons trade for 2006 to the voluntary UN Register of Conventional Arms, accounting for more than 535,000 weapons exported and 105,000 weapons imported. Some major arms-trading countries, such as Russia and the United States, have not provided information about their small arms commerce.

The UN register grew out of a 1991 agreement seeking to add transparency to the global arms trade, calling on all countries to report annually on their previous year's exports and imports. Historically, declarations have focused on heavy equipment such as tanks, combat aircraft, warships, large-caliber artillery, and missiles and missiles systems. Until this year, small arms and light weapons exports and imports, although much more numerous, were rarely included in countries' reports. For example, only a half-dozen countries had filed declarations at this time last year.

Of the 30 detailed declarations, most come from countries that are European, Western allies, and/or from the Western Hemisphere, skewing the findings to these states and their partners.

Data from the Register

The United Kingdom provided the longest small arms and light weapons report and ranks as by far the biggest exporter to file a declaration, with 359,444 of the 535,522 total reported weapons exported. The United Kingdom has filed small arms reports for the past four years and is a leader in the call for a global arms trade treaty.

Countries that were once part of the Warsaw Pact [a military treaty signed in 1955 between the former Soviet Union and a number of Soviet-bloc countries] account for three of the next four largest declared weapons exporters. Hungary claims 52,208 weapons exported, the Czech Republic 40,082 weapons exported, and Poland 25,591 weapons exported. Germany reports 29,179 weapons exported, ranking it fourth on the list.

Data does show that the United States is a key player in the small arms and light weapons trade even though it has not filed a detailed declaration.

Eastern European states are also major small arms importers. Georgia ranks first with 21,962 of the 105,317 total reported imported weapons. The Czech Republic and Bosnia and Herzegovina rank second and third with 16,514 and 14,470 weapons imported, respectively. Germany is fourth with 13,298 weapons imported. Canada is fifth with 10,877 weapons imported and Japan sixth with 6,605 weapons imported.

The data in the register also reveals trade by eastern European countries that did not themselves make small arms declarations. Austria did not include small arms in its register report, but 11 states claim to import small arms from the country. Similarly, Ukraine did not declare small arms, but Georgia reports the importation of 21,700 assault rifles from Ukraine.

To be sure, the reach of the register remains limited, and many experts recommended caution before drawing expansive conclusions. More than 70 countries have filed "nil" or not included small arms in their register declaration. There is almost no data regarding Africa. China's and Russia's declarations include heavier weapons but not smaller arms. Italy, Thailand, Saudi Arabia, and Spain rank among the top five importers or exporters of revolvers and pistols in 2006 by trade value according to the UN's Commodity Trade Statistics Database, but do not emerge as significant in the register.

No Filing from the United States

Data does show that the United States is a key player in the small arms and light weapons trade even though it has not filed a detailed declaration. Twelve countries report exporting to the United States, and 14 claim to be receiving U.S. imports. The United Kingdom claims that it exported more than 330,000 weapons to the United States, making the British-U.S. trade relationship the single largest in the register.

Still, absent a U.S. filing, small arms and light weapons numbers remain low in countries where the U.S. military is active. In the register, exports to Afghanistan come from Hungary, Slovakia, and the United Kingdom but account for less than seven percent of total weapons exported. Exports to Iraq come from Hungary, Poland, Turkey, and the United Kingdom and account for less than one percent of total weapons exported.

A U.S. official told *Arms Control Today* in September that the United States does intend to file a small arms report this year. The complexity of compiling records from various sources has slowed U.S. participation in this portion of the register, the official claimed. The United States has already filed for heavier weapons.

Small Arms and Light Weapons

In addition to being more numerous, the declarations this year are more detailed, perhaps due to an agreement reached last year to use a standard form comprised of six categories of small arms and seven of light weapons. The first two categories of small arms, consisting of revolvers and self-loading pistols, and rifles and carbines, account for more than 75 percent of total reported exports and imports. Additional small arms categories include assault rifles, sub- and light machine guns, and others.

Light weapons, which account for less than four percent of total claimed transfers, are defined as heavy machine guns, recoilless rifles, hand-held under-barrel and mounted grenade launchers, mortars of calibers less than 75 millimeters, portable anti-tank guns, missile launchers and rocket systems, and others. The register encourages reporting of civilian and military arms transfers, but not all countries appear to use the same standards.

Russia's Arms Trade Policies Are at Odds with U.S. Policies

Lionel Beehner

Lionel Beehner is formerly a senior writer for the Council on Foreign Relations, a nonpartisan membership organization promoting understanding of foreign policy choices facing the United States and other countries, which originally published the following viewpoint.

Last year [2005], Russia surpassed the United States as the developing world's leader in arms deals, according to a new report by the Congressional Research Service (CRS). But Russia has increased military shipments to anti-U.S. states like Iran and Venezuela, not to mention potential adversaries like China, which concerns U.S. policymakers far more. Experts say Iran—as well as Syria—may have transferred some of these small arms to groups like Hezbollah and Hamas. Also, Russia's arms relationship with Iran, the thinking goes, further complicates efforts to impose punitive sanctions against Tehran for its alleged pursuit of nuclear weapons.

Russia's Arms Sales to Iran

Since 1992, Russia has sold Iran hundreds of major weapons systems, including twenty T-72 tanks, ninety-four air-to-air missiles, and a handful of combat aircraft like the MiG-29. Late last year, Russia agreed to sell Iran a $700 million surface-to-air missile defense system (SA-15 Gauntlet) along with thirty TOR M-1 air-defense missile systems, ostensibly to defend its soon-to-be-complete, Russian-built nuclear reactor at Bushehr. Moscow also plans to upgrade Tehran's Su-24, MiG-29 aircraft, and T-72 battle tanks. Iran has shown interest in S-300 anti-aircraft missiles from Russia and Belarus, which can intercept enemy aircraft ninety to 180 miles away. Michael Eisenstadt, director of the Washington Institute for Near East Policy's Military and Security Studies Program, says Iran is building up its naval presence. In April 2006, the Iranians claimed to have tested a high-speed torpedo—similar to the Russian-made VA-111 *Shkval*—capable of destroying large warships or submarines. Iran already fields China's Silkworm anti-shipping missile and an array of mine technologies.

After the fall of the Shah in 1979, the Islamic Republic of Iran sought to secure itself by purchasing conventional arms mainly from China, North Korea, and, despite prickly bilateral relations, the Soviet Union (under the Shah, its chief supplier had been the United States and Britain). In 1989, following the death of Ayatollah Ruhollah Khomeini, Moscow and Tehran negotiated their first major arms deal along with agreements on scientific-technical cooperation, which included pledges of non-interference in each other's domestic affairs. Relations soon improved. By the end of the 1990s, once Iran's cooperation with North Korea had slowed, Russia emerged as Iran's main supplier of conventional arms. Between 1995 and 2000, Russia suspended its advanced weapons trade with Iran as part of a voluntary agreement with the United States. The value of arms transfer agreements between Iran and Russia ballooned from $300 million between 1998 and 2001 to $1.7 billion between 2002 and 2005.

During its month-long war with Hezbollah last summer [2006], Israel found Russian-made anti-tank weapons.

Some analysts see a quid pro quo ["something for something"] in place: Iran does not object to Russian interference in the predominantly Muslim Caucasus, while Russia refrains from agreeing to UN sanctions against Tehran. "However, for both parties, cooperation is driven as much by fear and mistrust as it is by opportunism and shared interests," wrote Eisenstadt in a March 2001 *Arms Control Today* article. According to Wade Boese, research director of the Arms Control Association, a Washington-based think tank, "Russia, like the United States, sees arms sales as a potential means of influence [over its buyers]." Finally, Russia's upsurge in arms sales with Iran is part of a concerted move by Moscow to expand its commercial reach to developing markets in the Middle East, Southeast Asia, and Latin America.

Concerns About Russia's Arms Trade with Iran

Do Iran's Russian-made arms pose a major security threat? They could, experts predict. "Sales of advanced military equipment to Iran by Russia and others has been an issue of intense interest to U.S. policymakers for some time," writes Richard F. Grimmett, author of the CRS report. "Iran appears to be interested in air-defense systems, which would pose a challenge to U.S. combat strikes in Iran," Boese says. Not all experts agree. "It's been a lot more smoke than fire," says Eisenstadt. "In terms of Iranian air defenses, [the Iranians are] still pretty weak given the size of the land mass they have to defend."

Does Iran funnel arms from Russia to terrorist groups? It's unclear. During its month-long war with Hezbollah last summer [2006] Israel found Russian-made anti-tank weapons, including RPG-29s, which proved highly effective against Israel's Merkava tanks. "It was largely the transfer of Iran's military technology and its asymmetric capabilities to Hezbollah that made it difficult for the high-tech-oriented Israeli military to 'eradicate' the fighting capabilities of that organization during the thirty-four-day war in July-August," writes Ehsan Ahrari, CEO of Strategic Paradigms, a Virginia-based defense consultancy, in the *Asia Times*. Most experts, however, say these rocket-propelled grenades were likely transferred to Hezbollah by Syria, not Iran. "It is very difficult for those of us looking from the outside to say with any certainty that Iran bought weapons from Russia and sold them to Hezbollah," says Matthew Schroeder, manager of the Federation of American Scientists' Arms Sales Monitoring Project. Part of the problem, he says, is that much of Russia's weaponry is widely proliferated, meaning that dozens of countries have imported it, and a number of them have produced their own variants, with and without Russia's consent. End-user agreements typically prohibit states from transferring arms to third parties; moreover, states are prohibited from funneling arms to Hezbollah by UN [United Nations] Security Council Resolution 1559, passed in 2004. Interestingly, experts point out that a major weakness in Hezbollah's capabilities demonstrated last summer was the group's lack of sophisticated air-defense missiles.

How important is the Iranian market to Russia's arms dealers? Not very, experts say, especially when compared to Russia's arms sales to China and India, which account for approximately two-thirds of Russia's arms shipments (Russia recently completed a deal to sell Beijing thirty Il-76TD transport aircraft and eight aerial refueling tankers, worth more than $1 billion). "Although Russia may see Iran as an attractive arms customer, I don't think we should inflate how important this market is to Russia," Boese says. Schroeder agrees that China and India remain Russia's most important customers. "If they lose them, they're in trouble," he says, but adds that Russia's "deals with Iran are pretty significant. We're talking hundreds of millions of dollars."

The United States' View of Russia's Arms Trade

How has Moscow's arms sales to Iran affected U.S.-Russian relations? They have added to already-strained relations, experts say. "As the U.S. focuses increasing attention on Iran's efforts to enhance its nuclear as well as conventional military capabilities, major arms transfers [from Russia] continue to be a matter of concern [among U.S. policymakers]," writes Grimmett in the CRS report. For their part, the Russians claim the arms they sell Iran are used for self-defense. "They see the United States as trying to diminish Russian arms sales and marketplace competition," Boese says. The trick from the Russians' perspective, adds Eisenstadt, "is to strike a balance in their foreign policy—supporting an Iran that can tie the U.S. down while not creating a Frankenstein that can threaten their own interests."

Does Russia's arms trade make efforts to sanction Iran more difficult? "It makes it harder but not impossible," Boese says of efforts to enlist Russian support for sanctions. "Moscow clearly has other cooperation with Iran that it sees as much more important than conventional arms sales and there is the general concern about embracing language or actions that could be seen as paving the way for U.S. military action against Iran." The larger issue for Moscow, he adds, is Bushehr and protecting Russia's financial stake there. Eisenstadt agrees, while adding that "there are more fundamental principles at stake here: the Russians want to delegitimize sanctions as an instrument of international diplomacy because they've been used against Moscow in the past."

What leverage does the U.S. have to limit Russian arms sales to Iran? Not much. "Part of the problem, in general, is there are no legal prohibitions to selling conventional weapons," Boese says, only voluntary—and thereby unenforceable— export-control regimes like the Missile Technology Control Regime or the Wassenaar Arrangement. Russia has come under criticism from the U.S. State Department for its lax compliance with these agreements. On its arms sales to Iran, "I imagine behind closed doors there are negotiations in Washington about it," Schroeder says, but adds that—like U.S. efforts to dissuade Russia from selling arms to Venezuela, including $3 billion of jet fighters and Kalashnikov assault rifles—they are unlikely to succeed. The United States can also sanction Russian entities for their alleged proliferation transactions with Iran. In total, the White House has slapped sanctions on six Russian firms for delivering arms-related materials to Iran, the most recent being Rosoboronexport and Sukoi this past September [2006]. Experts say these kinds of sanctions have little impact. Finally, the Russians might be willing to rescind their arms trade with Iran, says Eisenstadt, in exchange for American promises to block NATO [North Atlantic Treaty Organization] expansion eastward and to "stop meddling in [Russia's] near-abroad," something Washington appears unwilling to do.

China's Arms Trade in the Middle East Is Increasing

Stephen Pollard

Stephen Pollard is president of the Centre for the New Europe, a Brussels-based think tank. He is also a columnist with The Times, *a United Kingdom newspaper that is the source of the following selection.*

The story behind the story in the Middle East today is the proxy war, as Israel, on behalf of the US, takes on Hezbollah, which fights on behalf of Iran and Syria. Indeed, one can widen it further and describe the participants as proxies for the West versus militant Islam.

This analysis of the conflict sometimes mentions, in passing, Russia's declining influence. But there is another player that has somehow received almost no coverage.

China Cannot Be Ignored

For decades China has been building up influence in the Middle East. It suits China's strategy well that coverage has been almost non-existent. As Deng Xiaoping [former leader of the Communist Party of China] once put it, China must "hide brightness and nourish obscurity . . . to bide our time and build up our capabilities". As China develops into the role of global power, its influence on the region is no longer obscure; it cannot now be ignored.

The original postwar Middle East proxies were the US and the Soviet Union. Washington supporting Israel and the Kremlin sponsoring enemy regimes and their terrorist offshoots. But the Sino[Chinese]-Soviet split, which began in the 1960s, meant a lifting of the constraint on China getting involved, and it soon began to develop ties to countries that were not under Soviet influence, such as Egypt under [former President Anwar] Sadat.

A brilliant analysis of China's role by Barry Rubin, in the *Middle East Review of International Affairs*, describes China's first steps thus: "As hope for global revolution faded and Beijing switched its partners from tiny opposition groups to governments, China now projected itself as leader of the Third World, struggling against the hegemony of the two superpowers, the USSR and the United States. Lacking the strength and level of development of other great powers, China would try to make itself the head of a massive coalition of the weaker states." That meant, in the Middle East, Israel's enemies.

China's Need for Oil

Today countries such as Saudi Arabia, Iran, and Pakistan—all key states in the region—have strong ties to China, which they are all likely to see as a counterbalance to American power in the Middle East and beyond.

The Middle East is now China's fourth largest trading partner.

As President Jiang Zemin put it in 1994, US "hegemony" should be opposed, in part by helping countries such as Iran, which were already fighting that battle. But China's strategy dovetailed geopolitics with economic necessity. Without access to oil markets, China had to fuel economic expansion by turning to more neglected suppliers, such as Iran, Iraq and Sudan. And with a growing consumption of Gulf oil, so China has had to direct its security policy towards ensuring that the US will not be able to interfere with the flow of oil. This means developing ever stronger political and strategic relationships with oil exporters.

Jiang's state visit in 1999 to Saudi Arabia cemented what he termed a "strategic oil partnership". In 1996 Saudi exported 60,000 barrels per day to China. By 2000 exports stood 350,000 bpd [barrels per day] (17 per cent of Beijing's oil imports). Iranian oil exports rose even faster, from 20,000 bpd in 1995 to 200,000 bpd in 2000.

China's Trade Partners

The Middle East is now China's fourth largest trading partner. But its trade is hardly traditional. As Rubin puts it: "Being so late in entering the region—and having less to offer in economic or technology terms than the United States, Russia, Japan, and Europe—China must go after marginal or risky markets . . . supplying customers no one else will service with goods no one else will sell them." What that means, of course, is arms.

In the war-by-proxy analysis, Iran is rightly said to be the power and arms supplier behind Hezbollah. But the issue of where Iran's arms come from has been ignored. China has sold Iran tanks, planes, artillery, cruise, anti-tank, surface-to-surface and anti-aircraft missiles as well as ships and mines. It is also Iran's main supplier of unconventional arms and is thought by almost all monitors to be illicitly involved in supplying key elements in Iran's chemical and nuclear weapons programme. This is despite China being a signatory to the Nuclear Non-Proliferation Treaty and the Chemical Weapons Convention.

China has sold nuclear reactors to Algeria, Iran, Syria, and Saudi Arabia, and Chinese nuclear weapons designs were found in Libya. It has also negotiated with Syria on the sale of M11 ballistic missiles. China is one of the few global suppliers of ballistic missiles, and can charge a heavy price. It demanded of the Saudis, for instance, to whom it sold CSS2 missiles, payment in cash, ensuring both the cementing of a key strategic relationship and total deniability of the sale.

Both nations have kept the relationship as secret as possible, but one expert, Robert Mullins, estimates that at least 1,000 Chinese military advisers have been based at Saudi missile installations since the mid-1990s. Such secret deals are handled by Polytechnologies Incorporated, a defence firm controlled by the People's Liberation Army, which both installs weapons and trains handlers.

China's Lack of Principles

But like all the most successful illicit traders, China is ideologically profligate [reckless] in its relations. Keen to supply weapons to Israel's enemies in return for oil, it is equally happy to trade with Israel in return for its technology. As Benjamin Netanyahu put it to the Chinese when, as Prime Minister, he championed an Israeli investment in China: "Israeli knowhow is more valuable than Arab oil." The estimates are that there has been between $1 billion and $3 billion of arms trade between China and Israel. But in this case the flow of arms and weapons technology has been from Israel to China.

In the immediate analysis of the present conflict, it is clearly Iran and Syria that, as President [George W.] Bush put it, should "stop doing this shit." But any deeper explanation of the realpolitik of the Middle East has to include the insidious role of the Chinese, the 21st century's next superpower.

Israel Is a Significant Player in the Global Arms Trade

Odile Hugonot Haber

Odile Hugonot Haber is chair of the Women Challenging U.S. Policy: Building Peace on Justice in the Middle East Campaign.

Israel has a history of nurturing relations with Latin American militaries but alienating grassroots organizations and democratic movements that continues to this day.

Israel's Arms Trade History in Latin America

In the 1970s, Israel began selling weapons to Latin America under the aegis of the United States, explains Jane Hunter in her book *Israeli Foreign Policy: South Africa and Central America.* She writes:

> In 1973 Israel took orders from El Salvador for 18 Dassault Ouragan jetfighters aircraft. This was the first step, but then more weapons and military advice followed under the Reagan administration. Israel trained *contra* mercenary forces in Nicaragua and then expanded its mission to participate in the training for the rural "pacification" of the population of El Salvador, Guatemala, Nicaragua, Costa Rica, and Honduras, under the guise of an innovative technical assistance program.

Hunter defines rural "pacification" as "an attempt to suppress forever a people's ability to organize against an oppressive order."

Some were aware of the Israeli role in these operations, as in 1979 the FMLN (Farabundo Marti National Liberation

Odile Hugonot Haber, "Israeli Arms Sales: Latin America, China, and Beyond," *Peace & Freedom*, vol. 67, Fall 2007, pp. 6–7. Reproduced by permission.

Front) of El Salvador kidnapped Israel honorary consul Ernesto Liebes, executing him as a war criminal for facilitating the aircraft sale.

Israel started selling weapons to Guatemala in 1974, beginning with the Arava aircraft, followed by "RBY armored personnel carriers, patrol boats, light cannons, grenade launchers, machine guns, and 15,000 Galil assault rifles." Hunter continues, ". . . The aspect of Israeli cooperation with Guatemala which has the most serious implications is the role played by Israeli personnel in the universally condemned rural pacification program." In 1982, Israel military advisors had helped develop and conduct the devastating scorched-earth policy that General Rios Montt unleashed on the highland Maya population.

She then quotes the Guatemalan writer Victor Perrera: "Uzi and the larger Galil assault rifles used by Guatemala's counterinsurgency forces accounted for at least half of the estimated 45,000 Guatemalan Indians killed by the military since 1978."

The Nicaraguan *contra* leaders said they would obtain weapons from the Israeli embassy in Guatemala; sales also were made in Honduras. Hunter claims these sales were "made by Israeli arms dealers and the documents drafted by Honduras officials who made money on the transactions."

Of course, we recall Israel's important role in the Iran-contra scandal: Israeli officials were the intermediaries in the Reagan Administration's covert negotiations with Iran in the infamous arms-for-hostages deal.

Is Israel Washington's Proxy?

In the prologue of his book *Loose Cannon: On the Trail of Israel's Gunrunners in Central America*, author Jon Lee Anderson asked questions about the extent of the Israeli-American strategic partnership. "Is Israel acting as Washington's proxy in countries where Washington can't operate openly? What are the costs at home and abroad, in terms of international public opinion, of this 'Uzi diplomacy'?"

Writes Anderson: "Significant changes swept Central America in the 1970s in the form of social and political upheaval. Revolutionary movement broke out of quiescence in Nicaragua, El Salvador, and Guatemala, threatening the US-backed military regimes there and upsetting the status quo."

Israel's military influence in Latin America lives on.

He goes on, "Until 1982, a well-connected Israeli defense reporter told me ... arms sales were around $1 billion worldwide, since then it soared and arms sales have become a major strategic asset. The sale of Israeli know-how in counter terror, stressed the defense reporter, was also a big part of the business."

"A veteran Central American merchant sought to explain Israel's stratagems." Anderson explains, "Israel has a super production because of its own defense needs, and for Israel this implies a huge investment. Therefore, to sustain this, they have to sell somewhere; as far as Central America, it is an easy market for them."

Israel's Continuing Influence in Latin America

But Latin America is no longer the arms market it once was. According to the Arms Control Association, the region's arms imports "have generally accounted for roughly two to five percent of the world arms market [between 1992–2002]." However, Israel's military influence in Latin America lives on. As reported by many mainstream and alternative media, Carlos Castaño, the mysteriously disappeared leader of the Colombian paramilitary organization AUC (Autodefensorias Unidas de Colombia) was trained by Israel. AUC, identified by the U.S. State Department as a "foreign terrorist organization," has been accused of extensive human rights abuses and cocaine trafficking. Jeremy Bigwood, in his 2003 article for Al Jazeera, "Israel's Latin American Trail of Terror," explains:

> The AUC paramilitaries are a fighting force that originally grew out of killers hired to protect drug-running operations and large landowners. They were organized into a cohesive force by Castaño in 1997. . . . According to a 1989 Colombian Secret Police intelligence report, . . . Israeli trainers arrived in Colombia in 1987 to train him and other paramilitaries who would later make up the AUC. Fifty of the paramilitaries' 'best' students were then sent on scholarships to Israel for further training, according to a Colombian police intelligence report. . . .

Israel is now the fourth-largest global supplier of arms after the United States.

Bigwood further reports, "The Colombian AUC paramilitaries are always in need of arms, and it should come as no surprise that some of their major suppliers are Israeli."

Business Is Booming for Israel's Arms Trade

Meanwhile, the military/political marriage of Israel and the United States has continued. As military analyst Jonathan Reingold writes in an article on the website Commondreams.org, "U.S. Arms Sales to Israel End up in China, Iraq":

> From 1990 to 2000, U.S. military aid to Israel totaled over $18 billion. No other nation in the world has such a close relationship with the U.S. military and arms industries.

All told, Israel is now the fourth-largest global supplier of arms after the United States, and in 2006 Israel's defense exports hit a record high level. According to Israel's Defense Ministry, by the end of November 2006, arms firms had sealed

$4.1 billion in new foreign orders surpassing the previous peak—$4.02 billion—reached in the same period in 2002, writes Dan Williams in his article for Reuters, "Israel Arm Sales Peak Despite Lebanon War Fallout."

Israel is currently China's second-largest arms supplier; there is also ongoing cooperation between Israel and China under counter-terrorism programs. "Training programs for . . . China's People Liberation Army (PLA) representative and police at the Israeli Military Industries Academy for Advanced Security and Anti-terror Training are currently under discussions," states Dr. Eugene Kaplan in an article on Israelvalley-.com, the official website of the Chamber of Commerce Israel-France.

Beyond this, Israel's current weapons customers include Cambodia, Eritrea, Ethiopia, the South Lebanon army, India, Burma, and Zambia.

The Arms Trade Lacks Consistent National Controls

Debbie Hillier and Brian Wood

Experts on arms brokering and transporting, Debbie Hillier is with Oxfam Great Britain and Brian Wood is with Amnesty International. Both organizations are part of the Control Arms campaign.

While the world's attention is focused on the need to control weapons of mass destruction, the trade in conventional weapons continues unabated, with no global control. Both the state-sanctioned trade and the illicit trade in arms must be tackled, in order to prevent irresponsible use of arms and the horrific human cost that ensues.

The Arms Industry Is Unique

The monetary value of international authorised exports of arms is relatively small in global terms, amounting to around US$ 21 billion per year—representing half of one per cent of total world trade, and less than half of the value of the global coffee market. Yet these statistics completely belie the international significance of the arms trade. First, unlike other industries, many of the products manufactured and sold are specifically designed to kill and injure human beings. Second, the permanent members of the UN [United Nations] Security Council—China, France, the Russian Federation, the UK [United Kingdom], and the USA—are firmly entrenched in this business and profiting from it. In terms of financial value of conventional arms sales, in 2001 (the most recent year for which figures are available) they were the top five arms exporters in the world, together responsible for 88 per cent of conventional arms exports. The USA dominates the industry, contributing almost half (45 per cent) of all the world's exported weapons.

There are many ways in which the arms industry differs from others. According to Transparency International, the arms industry is the second most likely to involve bribes: a report from the US Department of Commerce claimed that the defence sector accounted for 50 per cent of all bribery allegations, even though it constitutes less than one per cent of all trade. Widespread corruption and questionable business practice are perhaps a result of the secrecy surrounding transactions, the complexity of contracts, and the fact that the industry is dominated by a small number of big deals. In addition, the industry often receives a much higher level of official subsidy, with governments actively promoting defence sales in a way unheard of in other sectors: high-ranking government ministers often lobby potential importers directly.

The profusion of arms-producing companies and nations presents a clear challenge to those who advocate strong controls.

The arms industry manufactures products and provides services which maim and kill. One would expect, therefore, a strong degree of control commensurate with this responsibility—governments and industry working together to ensure that these weapons are used and sold responsibly. Yet the arms trade is like no other, operating outside the jurisdiction of the World Trade Organization, the parameters of the UN Conference on Trade and Development (UNCTAD), and the bounds of the arms non-proliferation regime. The control is left to individual governments, which may be unwilling or unable to ensure responsible practices.

Production of Arms Is Uncontrolled

The Russian Federation has a large defence industry with centralised systems which should mean that exports can be relatively well controlled—yet there are no national legal criteria to ensure that weapons are not exported to destinations where they may be used for violations of international human rights and humanitarian law. In less well regulated economies, such as those of the many developing countries which produce arms, output is usually subject to even less stringent control.

Recent research has identified 1,135 companies manufacturing small arms and ammunition in at least 98 countries; these numbers are increasing all the time. Between 1960 and 1999, the number of countries producing small arms doubled, and there was an almost six-fold increase in the number of companies manufacturing them. While some of this increase can be explained by the privatisation of state industries, the creation of more nation states, and better reporting in the 1990s, the profusion of arms-producing companies and nations presents a clear challenge to those who advocate strong controls.

The absence of controls, together with the presence of loopholes or poor enforcement of controls, means that arms travel too easily around the world.

At the other end of the scale, domestic or 'craft' production of weapons is widespread in both developed and developing countries. Although the output is much smaller than that of official production, the impact in certain locations is highly significant.

Some of the weapons produced in this way are fairly basic: for example, pipe bombs in Northern Ireland, makeshift pistols made from bedsprings and metal tubing in Honduras and India, and grenades fired from home-made tubes cut from oil pipelines in Colombia. Other weapons are much more sophisticated, and sometimes of surprisingly high quality. The Palestinian group Hamas produces an anti-tank weapon called the 'Al Bana': a 95 mm rocket with a TNT warhead, fired from a plastic pipe one metre in length. In Colombia, the market is overloaded with *hechizas* (home-made weapons) of high quality at competitive prices, produced mainly in Cali and Pereira, and priced at approximately one third of the black-market original: a Walter PPK pistol might cost US$ 350 on the black market, but a home-made copy would cost only US$ 100. Most craft production involves guns, but rebel groups in Sri Lanka and Colombia have improvised tanks built from farm tractors or bulldozers, with cabs protected by armour plate and machine-guns mounted on top.

Lack of proper controls means that diversion of arms from the state-sanctioned sector to the illicit sphere is very common.

The absence of controls, together with the presence of loopholes or poor enforcement of controls, means that arms travel too easily around the world, reaching conflict zones and countries with poor human rights records or high levels of organised crime. The majority of weapons used in such situations are not home-produced. Arms, particularly small arms, do not respect national borders. One of the key features of the trade in arms is the way that weapons pass from the state-sanctioned sector to the illegal sphere. The boundary between the two is extremely weak and porous.

National Legislation Is Not Sufficient

National governments enact and enforce legislation to control the production, export, national sales, management, and use of arms. Too often these are woefully weak, riddled with loopholes, characterised by wide gaps between policy and practice—and as a result they allow easy access to lethal weaponry.

Because of links with national security and foreign policy, there is a broad international consensus that the export and import of arms should always be subject to authorisation by governments. Yet lack of proper controls means that diversion of arms from the state-sanctioned sector to the illicit sphere is very common. In addition, a government authorisation for sale may be influenced more by the economic or geopolitical importance of the deal than by any concerns over the subsequent impact of the arms, as the following examples show.

- As the Soviet Union fragmented, newly created states inherited arms-production facilities at a time when the need for foreign exchange and employment was a national priority over concerns over the use to which the arms would be put.

- More recently, in order for India to reach its goal of becoming a net exporter of arms, the government has chosen to abandon its arms-export blacklist.

- The Czech Republic, Slovakia, Bulgaria, Romania, and Poland, all modernising their systems and resources in preparation for NATO [North Atlantic Treaty Organization] membership, are dumping old Cold War tanks and heavy artillery on to the military market, making more weapons available for areas of violent conflict.

Responsible governments demand to see an *end-use certificate*, identifying the recipient of exported arms, and the purpose for which they are bought. In practice, diversion is common, because the system is easy to circumvent—either because of complacency on the part of the licensing body, or because of devious or corrupt practices in the production of the certificate. For example:

- Canadian government policy banned sales of arms to the Colombian military, on account of the risk that they might be used to violate human rights. However, a loophole in the law allowed 33 Canadian military helicopters to be sent to Colombia via the USA between 1998 and 2000. Canada does not require an end-use certificate for exports to the USA, and the USA provides no re-export guarantees.

- Despite assurances from Israel that 'no UK-originated equipment are [sic] used as part of the defence force's activities in the Territories', modified British Centurion tanks were used by Israeli troops in the West Bank and Gaza in 2002.

National Legislation Does Not Address Arms Brokering

Arms brokering, via third countries, is a key way by which arms get into the wrong hands. Brokers, supported by transporters and financiers, are middlemen who arrange transfers between sellers and buyers. Arms brokers, transporters, and financiers have been implicated in supplying weapons to the world's worst-affected conflict zones and human rights crisis zones, including those subject to embargoes by the UN—Afghanistan, Angola, DRC [Democratic Republic of the Congo], Iraq, Rwanda, Sierra Leone, and South Africa, to name but a few.

Most national arms-export legislation does not fully address the problem of international arms brokering, transporting, or financing; where legislation is in force, unscrupulous brokers may simply move 'off shore' to another country with weaker controls. Electronic banking and tax havens have made international movements of finance much easier to organise and more difficult to trace. Transporters avoid detection by flying planes on circuitous routes, via a number of airports, at night or at low altitudes to avoid radar; sometimes registration numbers are changed, and 'flags of convenience' are used.

Arms technology is exported when an arms company permits the production of its weapons in another country, under licence. The establishment of licensed production agreements in countries with a record of internal repression and human rights violations, or countries engaged in conflict, effectively circumvents export-control legislation that would not allow a direct transfer to that country. Often, the original manufacturer has little control once the agreement has been reached: the Bulgaria Arsenal plant continued to produce Kalashnikov rifles 14 years after its licensed production agreement had expired.

Small quantities of arms smuggled over borders by individuals (engaged in what is known as the 'ant trade') are often purchased lawfully and passed on to others. This occurs in Paraguay, where a tourist can, perfectly legally, buy two guns, providing opportunities for significant inflows of arms to neighbouring countries.

It is never right or good policy to sell arms to those who use them to commit atrocities.

Arms are recycled from one conflict to another, and from states with lax controls on civilian ownership. In late 2002, large stocks of surplus ammunition were flown from Albania—after an arms and ammunition collection exercise—to Rwanda, allegedly for use in eastern DRC. Countries torn apart by war, such as Afghanistan, Somalia, Angola and Albania, can be an easy source of illegal weapons.

The Failure to Prevent Irresponsible Arms Transfers

One of the major causes of the increasing availability of small arms in the world markets during the 1990s was the indiscriminate off-loading of standard weapons from members of the former Warsaw Pact [military treaty signed in 1955 between the former Soviet Union and Soviet-bloc countries] to poorer countries. Sometimes, this trend was accelerated by conversion to NATO standard weaponry.

When challenged on their failure to prevent irresponsible arms transfers, some governments have openly employed the morally flawed argument: 'If we don't sell them, someone else will'. When Tony Blair, UK Prime Minister, was asked why the UK was selling British parts for F16 aircraft for onward sale to Israel, when there had been clear evidence that these weapons were being used directly against civilians, he replied: 'What would actually happen if we [refused to sell parts] is not that the parts wouldn't be supplied, is that you would find every other defence industry in the world rushing in to take the place that we have vacated'. Even if this were true, it would not be morally right: it is never right or good policy to sell arms to those who use them to commit atrocities. The USA and the UK, among others, armed Iraq in the 1980s when there was clear evidence that the Iraqi government was guilty of violating the human rights of its own citizens. Why are these lessons from the past not being learned?

Often, powerful governments which profess to respect human rights and offer aid programmes to poor countries also authorise arms supplies which undermine the rule of law. For example, the UK is a key supplier of handguns to the Jamaican police force, which has one of the highest rates of police killings per capita in the world: 600 improperly investigated deaths since 1999. Small arms from Italy have been supplied to police and security forces in Algeria, Democratic Republic of Congo, Kenya, Nigeria, Sierra Leone, and Turkey, despite clear evidence of arms being used for excessive force, torture, and violations of human rights.

It is not arms production *per se* that is questionable, but the sale to irresponsible users, and the absence of controls to prevent arms reaching irresponsible users. The human cost of such sales is clear. Do arms producers really want the blood of civilians on their hands?

Inconsistent Laws and Management Lead to Problematic Arms Transfers

The national rules on firearm ownership for individuals vary widely from country to country, ranging from no control at all to a complete ban. Even the USA, the most heavily armed nation in the world, has many national and state laws to control the misuse of guns: for example, civilians are not allowed to buy military assault rifles. Yet such restrictions are often seriously inadequate: they contain significant loopholes, or they are not enforced. In Colombia, for example, even people with criminal records can easily obtain arms permits, if they bribe the relevant officials.

Those who are authorised users of weapons are often suppliers of weapons. There are many cases of police, military, and private security companies selling or hiring their arms for personal gain. In Colombia, rogue elements of the police obtain arms through confiscation and may try to sell them back to the original owners. In rural locations, such as some pastoralist areas of East Africa, the government may accept that it cannot provide security for its people, so it arms home-guards or police reservists, drawn from local populations, to protect their communities. People are seldom given adequate training or guidelines on how to use the weapons issued to them, and these arms are not usually provided equally to different ethnic groups, a fact which creates fear and tension.

Bad weapons management means that unauthorised users can acquire weapons. Huge quantities of arms are stolen from military or police depots. In Georgia, Russian stockpiles were looted systematically in 1991 and 1992, and those responsible were partly motivated by a belief that such actions were officially sanctioned as Soviet property became nationalised. Arms are stolen from licensed shops and private individuals; in South Africa, where the two major sources of illegal firearms are loss and theft from licensed firearm owners and the state, 80 guns a day were reported lost or stolen in 1998. In the Solomon Islands, the Malaita Eagle Force twice raided police armouries in 2000, obtaining enough M-18 assault rifles to commit, with police complicity, widespread violations of human rights against unarmed civilians from Guadalcanal Island.

During conflict, arms pass between warring parties as territory is won and lost, arms stores are captured and recaptured, and arms are abandoned on the battlefield. For many months, arms from Taliban caches discovered by US forces in Afghanistan were distributed freely to local militia. As conflicts come to a close and peace agreements are signed, arms are often not collected from combatants and removed from society; instead, they move into civilian ownership; this was markedly the case in and around Mozambique and Cambodia. In Bosnia, seven years after the end of the war and after extensive weapons-collection exercises, NATO peacekeepers have said that most households possess some wartime weapon. One million illegal weapons are still circulating in the Balkans region.

It is clear that the lack of controls means that arms too easily get into the hands of those who use them to violate international human rights and humanitarian law—whether the abuser is an agent of a repressive government, a criminal, a violent husband, or a member of an armed political group. Some of the methods of transfer described above are 'legal' under the national laws of the states involved—because a law to control the transfer either does not exist or it has loopholes; but the fact that transfers are not banned does not make them morally right, and they may well be unlawful according to international law.

Arms Are Traded Routinely in Spite of Embargoes

Oliver Sprague

Oliver Sprague is Amnesty International UK's Arms Programme director. Amnesty International, along with Oxfam and the International Action Network on Small Arms, runs the Control Arms campaign, which calls for a global, legally binding arms trade treaty to reduce the human suffering caused by irresponsible transfers of conventional weapons and munitions.

D espite the fact that every one of the 13 United Nations [UN] arms embargoes imposed in the last decade has been systematically violated, only a handful of the many arms embargo breakers named in UN sanctions reports has been successfully prosecuted. According to the Stockholm International Peace Research Institute, between 1990 and 2001 there were 57 separate major armed conflicts raging around the globe, yet only eight of them were subject to UN arms embargoes.

UN Arms Embargoes

Such embargoes are usually late and blunt instruments, and the UN Sanctions Committees, which oversee the embargoes, have to rely largely on Member States to monitor and implement them. Therefore, arms embargoes cannot be deployed effectively as an instrument by the UN to prevent illicit arms trafficking, without better national controls on international arms transfers. These controls are woefully inadequate.

Oliver Sprague, "UN Arms Embargoes: An Overview of the Last Ten Years," London, U.K.: Amnesty International, The International Action Network on Small Arms, and Oxfam at www.controlarms.org, 2006. Copyright © 2006 Amnesty International Publications, 1 Easton Street, London WC1X 0DW, U.K., The International Action Network on Small Arms, and Oxfam International. Reproduced with the permission of Oxfam GB, Oxfam House, John Smith Drive, Cowley, Oxford OX4 2Jy U.K., www.oxfam.org.uk, and Amnesty International, www.amnesty.org. Oxfam GB does not necessarily endorse any text or activities that accompany the materials, nor has it approved the adapted text.

In addition, the Sanctions Committees of the Security Council have to rely on UN investigative teams and UN peace-keeping missions to investigate violations of embargoes and report compliance. However, these bodies usually have inadequate resources and time to do that work thoroughly.

There are currently [as of March 2006] UN mandatory territorial arms embargoes in force against the Ivory Coast, Liberia and Somalia. Non-state actors (rebel groups and their leaders) are also subject to arms embargoes. Currently, every state in the international community is prohibited from transferring arms to such non-state actor groups in the Democratic Republic of Congo (DRC), Liberia, Rwanda, Sierra Leone and in Sudan, as well as to Al-Qaida and associated persons.

In the last decade, there have also been embargoes imposed on Angolan armed rebels (1992 to 2002), Ethiopia and Eritrea (2000 to 2001), Iraq (1990 to 2003), Libya (1992 to 2003), and the former Yugoslavia (1991 to 1996 and again from 1998 to 2001). None of these mandatory UN arms embargoes has stopped the supply of arms; sometimes the embargoes have made it logistically more difficult and expensive to acquire the desired arms, but available evidence suggests that on the whole violations of UN arms embargoes appear persistent, widespread and systematic.

Countries Involved in Violating Embargoes

Private individuals who are arms dealers, brokers, financiers and traffickers, as well as companies around the world, have been involved in embargo busting, usually working in networks. A sample of UN Panel of Expert reports on embargoed destinations in Africa shows that companies and individuals based in the following wide range of countries have facilitated the supply of arms to embargoed destinations over the last decade. The list includes countries of manufacture, export, import, transit, diversion and company registration involved in the illegal deals. This is by no means an exhaustive list but shows the global nature of trafficking networks:

Albania, Belgium, the British Virgin Islands, Bulgaria, Burkina Faso, Burundi, the Cayman Islands, Cyprus, Egypt, Gibraltar, Guinea, Israel, Liberia, Libya, Moldova, Nigeria, Romania, Russia, Rwanda, Serbia, South Africa, the Ivory Coast, Togo, Uganda, Ukraine, United Arab Emirates, United Kingdom, Zimbabwe.

Given the clandestine nature of arms deliveries to embargoed destinations, it is impossible to quantify precise volumes of weapons deliveries to these countries.

Additionally, weapons and munitions recovered by UN personnel in embargoed destinations have been traced back to their country of manufacture. Whilst again this is not an exhaustive list, these countries include:

Belgium, Bulgaria, China, Germany, Egypt, Romania, Russia, Serbia, Ukraine.

The origins of these weapons have been identified from serial numbers and other relevant markings but sometimes UN personnel fail to record the relevant markings to enable the supply chain to be traced. Some of these arms may have been supplied before an embargo was imposed, or may have been diverted from third-country stockpiles, so even an analysis of serial numbers doesn't always imply a breach of sanctions by the original manufacturing country. Investigators also have to look for documentary and other evidence in many countries but do not have the time and resources to do so. UN and other data also indicates that older, second hand, surplus weapons and ammunition are often transferred to embargoed destinations in large quantities, but not identified by UN field missions.

How Many Weapons Get Through the System?

Given the clandestine nature of arms deliveries to embargoed destinations, it is impossible to quantify precise volumes of weapons deliveries to these countries. However, it is clear from the few cases that UN experts have reported, that the scale of arms deliveries is extremely significant. Analysis of documents, including copies of end-user certificates (EUCs), and freight documents from several case studies identified in various UN investigative reports, shows that a typical delivery can contain several million rounds of ammunition, tens of thousands of assault rifles, machine guns and pistols, and thousands of grenades and rocket-propelled grenades. For example, a Serbian company, Temex, delivered nearly 210 tonnes of weapons to Liberia in mid-2002. The UN details a series of six flights between 1 June and 31 August 2002, with weapons equating to approximately

- five million rounds of ammunition

- 5160 assault rifles, pistols and machine guns

- 4500 hand grenades

- 6500 mines

- 350 missile launchers

These shipments alone include enough bullets to kill the entire population of Liberia. A consignment of five million rounds of ammunition is approximately enough to keep an armed group of 10,000 fighters supplied for a whole year.

Basic Flaws in the UN Embargo System

UN arms embargoes are imposed as a method of last resort, usually once the humanitarian and human rights situation in a particular country has already reached crisis point. Decisions to impose, or more importantly not to impose arms embargoes, are also largely guided by political considerations. Often the commercial, political or other strategic interests of any one member of the UN Security Council means a decision to impose an arms embargo on a particular regime or armed group is not tabled or agreed.

UN arms embargoes are also routinely and systematically violated because Member States, especially powerful states, do not support the UN with proper enforcement. For example, despite UN mandatory arms embargoes being legally binding under the UN Charter, many states have not even made violating an embargo a criminal offence in domestic law. UN investigative teams tasked with monitoring the embargoes are given woefully inadequate resources and time to do their difficult job given the inherently clandestine nature of such traffic and its grave consequences.

Unfortunately, very rarely do embargo busters get caught red handed with illegal weapons in a country subject to a UN arms embargo. Dealers and traffickers are adept at plying the weaknesses in national control systems to find a way of getting their weapons into these destinations. Typically, the individuals behind these deals will set up a labyrinth of front companies, make frequent use of fraudulent or misleading official paperwork, utilise a myriad of shipping companies' freight forwards and handling agents, and hide payments via offshore banking and financial services. They may also route the actual deliveries via third countries (not subject to embargo restrictions) and create such a complex supply chain that any individual element can deny knowledge of deliberate attempts to violate international arms embargoes. This deliberate obfuscation creates a web of deceit akin to 'an international get-out-of-jail-free card.'

Moreover, state officials often cover up arms transfers when providing information to the UN investigators because of narrow political interests, corruption or ignorance. UN peacekeepers collecting weapons and munitions belonging to embargoed entities are sometimes not trained to adequately record markings, while UN missions do not have adequate means to monitor ports of entry in embargoed zones. Charter aircraft and cargo firms that are repeatedly used to break UN arms embargoes are often not grounded or closed down—when exposed by the UN the owners can easily switch their registrations and company names, so the same trafficking networks continue to ply their deadly trade.

The European Union Struggles to Establish Effective Arms Trade Controls

Helen Hughes

Helen Hughes is an arms control researcher for Amnesty International.

The European Union [EU] is a major player in the global arms trade, with almost a third of the world market. How has it managed to maintain this share despite fierce competition from the United States, China and Russia, while developing a novel regional approach to control of the export of conventional arms?

European governments gradually began to recognise the links between arms exports and human rights, development, security and stability.

France, Germany, Italy, Sweden and Britain are among the top 10 largest arms suppliers. Between 1994 and 2001 the EU exported nearly $10bn [billion] of arms to developing countries—approximately one-third of all deliveries to such countries. Strong government support for some large deals has enabled many EU countries to compete in a market dominated by the US.

The History of EU Arms Control

EU enlargement in 2004 has increased the scope and number of companies producing and exporting military and dual-use equipment, with more than 400 companies in 23 out of the

Helen Hughes, "Europe's Deadly Business," *Le Monde Diplomatique*, June 2006. Copyright © 1997-2008 *Le Monde Diplomatique*. This article reprinted from *Le Monde Diplomatique*'s English language version, available online at www.mondediplo.com. Reproduced by permission.

25 EU countries producing small arms and light weapons, in total slightly fewer than in the US. Enlargement means opportunities and dangers for European arms control.

During the cold war the focus of arms control, nonproliferation and disarmament was on nuclear weapons and major systems. The road to responsible arms exports began with the end of the cold war, when states began to recognise the need for restrictive policies when selling arms abroad. Before then, cold war allegiances determined who would receive western European arms exports, and sympathetic dictators such as Suharto (Indonesia), Galtieri (Argentina) and Idi Amin (Uganda) benefited. After Iraq's invasion of Kuwait in August 1990 and the involvement of many European states in the Gulf war, it became clear that arms exports could affect regional stability and security, and might be used against the armed forces of supplier states or their allies. The British arms for Iraq affair, which revealed that Britain had knowingly allowed the supply of arms to Saddam Hussein, led to the reform of Britain's export control regime a decade later.

European governments gradually began to recognise the links between arms exports and human rights, development, security and stability. This was partly the result of pressure from human rights, humanitarian and other NGOs [nongovernmental organizations], such as Amnesty International (AI), which had documented the human costs of irresponsible arms transfers. There was public outrage over conflicts in Africa and the Balkans, and over rights abuses in East Timor/ Indonesia, Myanmar, Saudi Arabia and Turkey, which involved the types of military police equipment delivered by European countries.

Cooperation on conventional weapons has advanced among member states since the early 1990s, primarily in developing responsible export policies. In June 1991 the European Council agreed seven criteria to be taken into account in national decisions on arms exports, and in 1992 added an eighth. In June 1997 the Council agreed a programme to prevent and combat illicit trafficking in conventional arms. A year later the Council adopted the EU code of conduct on arms exports, a significant advance in regional control. AI, Oxfam, Saferworld and other NGOs pressured governments for more control of the trade.

Despite promises, member states have allowed arms and security equipment to be transferred to human rights abusers.

Criteria in the EU Code of Conduct

The 1998 EU code was the first regional initiative to attempt to harmonise the regulation of the trade. Member states committed themselves to "set high common standards" as the minimum criteria governments would use to "prevent the export of equipment which might be used for internal repression or international aggression, or contribute to regional instability". These criteria are the cornerstone of the agreement:

1. Respect for international commitments.
2. Respect of human rights and international humanitarian law in the country of final destination.
3. The internal situation of the country of final destination.
4. Preservation of regional peace, security and stability.
5. The national security of member states, of territories whose external relations are the responsibility of a member state, and of friendly and allied countries.
6. The buyer country's behaviour towards the international community, especially its attitude to terrorism, the nature of its alliances and respect for international law.

7. The risk that the equipment will be diverted within the buyer country or re-exported under undesirable conditions.

8. The compatibility of the arms exports with the technical and economic capacity of the recipient country.

The code requires member states to use one or more of these to consider, on a case-by-case basis, requests for exports of military equipment, including small arms, light weapons and dual-use equipment. When deciding to issue a licence, officials need to consider, for example, whether there is a risk that the equipment might be used for internal repression or undermine the development of the recipient country. (European suppliers, including Germany, France, Sweden and Britain, have made a major deal with South Africa, covering frigates, submarines, aircraft and helicopters, worth $6bn at 2003 prices; this far exceeds the state's spending on other projects, such as combating HIV/Aids at $53.8m [million] a year.)

These criteria are complemented by provisions that oblige states to inform each other about licences refused ("denial notifications") and circulate an annual report on their implementation of the code.

Member States Have Not Followed the Code

Despite these commitments, some member states have, wittingly or not, undermined, bypassed or ignored national export criteria and the EU code. Despite promises, member states have allowed arms and security equipment to be transferred to human rights abusers. Spain and other countries (including the US and Britain) have authorised in recent years transfers of equipment and other assistance to Colombia. Given the human rights violations committed by Colombian security forces and paramilitaries associated with them, such transfers are contrary to the code.

Italian-made small arms have also been transferred to countries in conflict or where violations of human rights and humanitarian law occur, including Algeria, Colombia, Eritrea, Indonesia, India, Israel, Kazakhstan, Nigeria, Pakistan and Sierra Leone. The ambiguous wording of the criteria allows for widely differing interpretations: tighter language, consistent with international law, would help prevent member states from making irresponsible export licensing decisions.

To prevent the problem of one state denying a license and another authorising it, EU states agreed to notify each other of licences refused because a proposed export failed to meet the criteria. But since the final decision remains with individual states, this has not always stopped exports. In 2002 Germany refused to sell rifles to the Nepalese government. Then there were reports that the Royal Nepalese Army was using Hechler & Koch rifles, and concerns that the German company Hechler & Koch, which had a longstanding licensed production arrangement with a British company, Royal Ordnance, had passed the contract on. Since there is no German transparency over such deliveries, AI has not been able to ascertain whether the rifles were exported to Nepal directly or indirectly from Germany and/or Britain. Soon after, the Belgian government agreed to supply Nepal with 5,500 light machine-guns (LMG), although Belgium is subject to the code; it is reported that some 3,000 out of 5,500 Minimi LMGs ordered from the Fabrique Nationale factory in Herstal, Belgium, were delivered to Nepal.

Loopholes, Weaknesses, and Omissions in the Code

Problems with the EU code are not confined to the application of the criteria. Loopholes, weaknesses and omissions mean that arms are still slipping through the net. The Dutch government has failed to bring the huge transit trade in arms through the Netherlands under its export policy, allowing armoured vehicles to be shipped to Israel despite Israeli security forces having used such vehicles to kill and injure civilians. Czech and Polish surplus weapons have been authorised for transfer to governments such as Yemen which have poor end-use controls and a history of diversion. Danish shipping companies have been allowed to transport arms to Myanmar, China and Sudan, which are under EU embargoes and have persistent human rights violations. A German technology company supplied phone-tapping and surveillance equipment to Turkmenistan, with its long history of repression. French helicopters and parts, manufactured under licence in India, were delivered to Nepal, where forces have previously shot civilians from helicopters.

The gaps and weaknesses in the code must be tackled. Controls must be extended to cover all arms and security equipment, technology and components, and to include licensed production, brokering, transporting, financing, expertise and services of arms to ensure these do not contribute to human rights violations or breaches of humanitarian law. Definitions in the code must explicitly cover the transit trade and the trade in surplus weapons.

At present the code is not a legally binding instrument and not all member states have introduced it into their national laws. The code will become a common position, which will give it legal status, but will not oblige individual member states to enact its criteria and provisions into their own national laws. The debate about strengthening the code (in the first review since it was agreed in 1998) has become entangled in a separate debate on lifting the EU arms embargo against China.

Although that embargo has been in force since June 1989, some EU countries have continued to sell equipment to China. The embargo does not specify which equipment is covered, so many countries have interpreted it differently. France reportedly approved a proposal by the company Thales Angenieux to set up a licensed arms production facility with North Night Vision Technology Co Ltd in Beijing to produce night-vision goggles, which can be assembled to military specifications. The British government, which intreprets the embargo more narrowly, refused a licence for image intensifiers from Pyser SGI. France has led calls to lift the embargo. But not all states agree with this, and the US government has exerted pressure for the embargo to stay.

Because of the scale of its arms industry, the EU has a specific obligation to stop irresponsible arms transfers.

The UK Working Group on Arms, made up of British NGOs, which has followed the debate, claims that "developments in strengthening the EU export control regime have been held hostage to embargo discussions, which have themselves stalled".

The EU Code Is Not Enough

The most significant revisions of the code have been the inclusion of the words "international humanitarian law" and the further elaboration of the criteria. Under the EU Council working group responsible for arms export controls, practical guidelines have been developed to assist officials responsible for deciding whether to authorise an arms export under criterion 8. There is now work to provide guidance for officials on criteria 2 and 7. This should clarify and harmonise interpretation across EU member states.

While the code has had a big impact on the arms export policy of EU states, governments still allow exports that can be used to fuel armed conflict, exacerbate human rights abuses and undermine development. Because of the scale of its arms industry, the EU has a specific obligation to stop irresponsible arms transfers. But regional control approaches are not enough. A global trade needs global control. The solution, sought by NGOs including the Control Arms Campaign, is a global arms trade treaty based on international law, which would ensure that all states abide by the same rules and standards. It would help to develop clarity and consistency across the national export control regimes.

The European Council has acknowledged the growing world support for such a treaty to establish common standards for the global trade in conventional arms. EU countries, including Denmark, Finland, France, Germany, Greece, Spain and Britain have made statements in support. To help overcome fundamental problems with the EU arms control regime, member states should support the development of a treaty. This would help strengthen the EU code's export criteria; but unlike the code, it could be ratified and implemented by many more states worldwide. Work needs to start at the latest by the end of this year. The EU can help make this happen.

CHAPTER 2

Does the Arms Trade Increase Security?

Chapter Preface

Given the potential negative and deadly consequences of irresponsible arms transfers around the globe, and the fact that weapons can be used to maim and kill not just legitimate enemies but innocent civilians, the arms industry is frequently pressed to justify its actions. One such justification for arms production and trade is that weapons and military technology are needed by countries to increase security. This is certainly one of the justifications given for the United States' arms trade with Israel—that providing arms to Israel contributes to Israeli security, which is in the security interests of the United States.

The United States is the primary source of Israel's military arsenal. Between 1996 and 2005, the United States delivered more than $10 billion of weaponry and military equipment to Israel, which includes both direct commercial sales and acquisitions through the foreign military (government-to-government) sales program. For some, the controversial nature of the United States' arms trade with Israel is exacerbated by the fact that the U.S. government gives direct monetary aid to Israel, providing them with a certain percentage of their military budget, which is then used to buy arms.

The relationship between the United States and Israel began with U.S. support for the creation of a Jewish homeland in 1948, after World War II. The United States has had many interests in the Middle East since then, including the prevention of Soviet expansion during the Cold War and ensuring access to the vast petroleum resources in the region. Since the establishment of Israel, the boundaries of the country and even the right of the country to exist have been disputed by Israel's Arab neighbors. There have been a series of wars in the region, and though Israel has signed peace treaties with Egypt and Jordan, the dispute with Palestinians continues today. The Palestinians lay claim to several areas within Israel—most notably the West Bank, Gaza Strip, and East Jerusalem—and Palestinians and others have been fighting for a Palestinian state for decades. Both Israel and the United States claim to share the goal of peace between Israel and its Arab neighbors, but how best to achieve this peace is a matter of intense debate.

Despite the fact that Israel is often seen as the United States' closest ally in the Middle East, this has not prevented the United States from attempting to develop alliances with other countries in the region. These relationships, such as those with Bahrain, Egypt, Iraq, Jordan, Kuwait, Oman, Saudi Arabia, and United Arab Emirates (U.A.E.), have often included military assistance or arms transfers.

There is no consensus on the issue of whether arms transfers to Israel and other countries in the Middle East increase security, both for the countries themselves and the United States. Whereas some argue that it is important to keep certain countries armed in order to prevent other countries in the region from attacking, others maintain that there is a dangerous arms race occurring in the Middle East that threatens security for the entire world. The viewpoints in this chapter address the question of whether the arms trade increases or decreases world security.

The Arms Trade in the Middle East Will Lead to Greater Stability

Anthony H. Cordesman

Anthony H. Cordesman holds the Arleigh A. Burke Chair in Strategy at the Center for Strategic and International Studies (CSIS), a nonprofit organization that conducts research and develops policy initiatives. He is also a national security analyst for ABC News.

In an ideal world, arms sales are hardly the tool the United States would use to win stability and influence. America does not, however, exist in an ideal world, nor in one that it can suddenly reform with good intentions and soft power. Those pressuring Congress to kill the Bush administration's proposed $20 billion arms deal with Saudi Arabia and other Gulf states need to step back into the real world.

Saudi Arabia's Importance as a U.S. Ally

America has vital long-term strategic interests in the Middle East.

The gulf has well over 60 percent of the world's proven conventional oil reserves and nearly 40 percent of its natural gas. The global economy, and part of every job in America, is dependent on trying to preserve the stability of the region and the flow of energy exports.

Washington cannot—and should not—try to bring security to the gulf without allies, and Saudi Arabia is the only meaningful military power there that can help deter and contain a steadily more aggressive Iran. (Disclosure: the nonprofit organization I work for receives financing from many sources, including the United States government, Saudi Arabia and Israel. No one from any of those sources has asked me to write this article.) We need the support of the smaller gulf states as well, but Saudi Arabia underpins any effort at regional security cooperation and in dealing with Iranian military adventures and acquisition of nuclear weapons.

This means mutual tolerance and respect. Saudi Arabia is not the United States, and reform there is going to be slow and often focused more on economic development and the quality of governance than on democracy and human rights. Reform, however, does happen. Saudi cooperation in counter-terrorism still has limits, but it has steadily improved. For all the rather careless talk about Saudi nationals entering Iraq to fight a jihad, the numbers of volunteers total some 10 to 25 a month.

Until we wake up in a perfect world, we must build strong security relations with allies that are sometimes less than perfect.

Moreover, the United States is in a poor position to criticize Saudi support of its positions in Iraq and the Arab-Israeli peace process. Sunni Arabs like the Saudis have every reason to accuse the Bush administration of being slow to realize it was backing a political process in Iraq that has led to the broad sectarian "cleansing" of Sunnis in key cities like Baghdad and that has so far deprived them of a fair share of political power and Iraq's wealth.

Until the last few months, when the administration suddenly rediscovered the importance of the Arab-Israeli peace process, Saudi Arabia was pushing harder for a deal than Washington was.

Arms Sales to the Middle East Are Important

Critics of the Saudi arms deal have also taken aim at the administration's proposed increases in military aid to Israel and Egypt. That, too, is misguided. The success of Israel's peace with Egypt and Jordan is heavily dependent on American military aid to Egypt.

Israel itself faces new threats and must maintain its conventional military edge; it must adapt to new asymmetric threats from Iran, Syria and Hezbollah, and it has to deal with the growing possibility of an Iranian nuclear threat to its very existence. Helping Israel deal with conventional threats through arms sales frees it to deal with those other threats on its own, and produces far more stability in the region than would a weak Israel, which might have to strike pre-emptively or overreact.

Equally important, the proposed arms sales are not going to produce sudden shifts in the military balance or a new regional arms race.

While the scope of the Israel deal—more than $30 billion over the next 10 years—seems huge, it really means deliveries over a decade at a cost one-third higher than in the past. Given the steadily rising cost of arms technology, Israel may not "break even" in terms of actual numbers of weapons delivered. Egypt will get substantially less down the road, but enough to show that it has parity in some key types of weapons and to be a significant potential partner in any future broader regional struggle.

Sales to Saudi Arabia will take place with or without the United States—from Europe, Russia or China. It will take more than a decade for the weapons to be delivered and fully absorbed into Saudi forces.

They will help the kingdom deal with a growing Iranian missile threat, give it the precision-strike capability that can deter Iranian adventures, and update Saudi forces that have lagged in a number of important areas.

Until we wake up in a perfect world, we must build strong security relations with allies that are sometimes less than perfect. We also must not discriminate between Israel and Arab allies, which would undercut our national interest and maybe actually weaken Israeli security by increasing Arab hostility to both Israel and the United States. This is particularly true when the motive for such discrimination is domestic political posturing and self-advantage, rather than a serious concern for America's role in the world.

U.S. Arms Trade with Taiwan Is Important for Its Defense

John J. Tkacik Jr.

John J. Tkacik Jr. is a senior research fellow in Asian studies at the Heritage Foundation, and a retired diplomat who served overseas with the U.S. Foreign Service in Taiwan, Iceland, Hong Kong, and China.

After four years of complaining that Taiwan hasn't bought the advanced weapon systems that the Bush administration approved in April 2001, the State Department appears unwilling now, at long last, to take "yes" for an answer.

State Department Opposition

In June [2007], Taiwan's Legislative Yuan finally approved multiyear procurement of P-3 Orion submarine hunter aircraft (about $1.3 billion), the Patriot PAC-2 GEM anti-ballistic missile batteries (another $800 million), and some additional small change for a submarine "feasibility study" ($6 million).

Taiwan's letters of request (LoRs) are at the Pentagon. As a bonus, Taiwan's lawmakers approved start-up funding for 66 new F-16C/D fighter jets to replace aging F-5s. The fighter replacement program would be about $3.5 billion. Pentagon officials (not to mention defense contractors) were ecstatic. But not the State Department.

State Department officers now tell the Pentagon they don't want the package to move. They say they fear approving the package might "embolden" Taiwan's president to move ahead with a local referendum on Taiwan's entry into the United Nations.

(It is an inconvenient truth, however, that public pressure for the "referendum" convinced even Taiwan's opposition par-

John J. Tkacik Jr., "Approve Taiwan Arms Buy; Don't Let China Dictate U.S. Policy," *Defense News*, July 30, 2007. Reproduced by permission.

ties that continuing to block defense funds would lose them votes in next January's election, so delaying the Taiwan defense package isn't likely to "embolden" Taiwan's polity any more than it already is).

Internally, State Department officials acknowledge that the eagerness of Christopher Hill, assistant secretary of state, to get something concrete out of his North Korean denuclearization efforts means he will not entertain any policy decision that might anger Beijing. And Taiwan weapon sales are a surefire way for the State Department to get an agitated visit from the Chinese ambassador.

Taiwan remained one of America's top defense customers into 2006.

Taiwan Is a Top Arms Customer

Taiwan's LoRs for the P-3s and the PAC-2 GEM have been in the Pentagon for weeks. The Pentagon has prepared the congressional notification package and now awaits the green light from the State Department to notify Congress (it needs a 20-day informal and 30-day formal notification period, after which the contract packages go to Taiwan for signature and the funds).

Unhappily, so much time has passed since President Bush's April 2001 approval of a multibillion-dollar "Big Bang" arms package that the U.S. bureaucracy has gotten out of the habit of moving Taiwan defense cases. A $750 million package of Kidd-class destroyers (part of the Big Bang list) was approved in 2002; a $1.8 billion phased-array ABM radar package was approved in 2004.

In fact, despite the delays in some Big Bang purchases, Taiwan remained one of America's top defense customers into 2006. And in March, the Bush administration approved a $400 million contract for Taiwan air-to-air missiles—seemingly pushed by the Pentagon—over State Department objections, as a demonstration of American anger at China's anti-satellite weapon test in January.

The U.S. Cannot Let China Dictate Policy

But if the Bush administration is to avoid giving Beijing a veto over America's strategic relationships in Asia (like Taiwan, Japan is facing similar resistance from the State Department in its request for the F-22 fighter), it must rebuild its military ties with key Asian allies. Notifying Congress of the Taiwan P-3 Orion and PAC-2 GEM missile defense batteries— and moving on Taipei's request for more F-16s—would be a start.

"The key," one anonymous administration official told me, "is to move the existing [Taiwan] cases, we [must] now get them notified to the Hill; the PRC [People's Republic of China] is going to scream, but then they always scream."

The trick, he said, is to "get everybody back into the habit of approving Taiwan arms sales." Once that's done, he observed, "then we can move with the F-16s ... but people in Taiwan know that's the dynamic ... the F-16 money isn't going to be available after September."

Taiwan's pro-China politicians cleverly stipulated the F-16 money would be canceled after Oct. 1 if the U S. failed to respond.

A package of 66 new F-16C/Ds for Taiwan, worth about $4 billion, is absolutely essential to keeping Taiwan's Air Force credible in the Strait. Taiwan's 250 aging F-5Es are at the end of their 25-year service lives and must be replaced. Holding up their approval because of anxieties about China is—arguably—illegal.

Selling Arms to Taiwan Is Required

In the Taiwan Relations Act of 1979, Congress specifically mandated that the "President and the Congress shall deter-mine the nature and quantity of such defense articles and services based solely upon their judgment of the needs of Taiwan." There is no room for the administration to debate the definitions of the words "shall" or "solely." "Shall" means it must be done, and "solely" means the administration may not, under any circumstances, consider China's reactions to the sale of any given defense package to Taiwan.

President Reagan insisted in 1982 that "it is essential that the quantity and quality of the arms provided Taiwan be conditioned entirely on the threat posed by the PRC. Both in quantitative and qualitative terms, Taiwan's defense capability relative to that of the PRC will be maintained."

Reagan termed this concept "a permanent imperative of U.S. foreign policy."

This raises grave questions about the Bush administration's Asia policy. Are Washington's defense sales to key U.S. allies in Asia being held hostage to China's preferences? China is the rising military power in the Western Pacific, a fact appreciated all too well in Tokyo and Taipei.

Washington can play with its diplomacy in other areas, but it must not sacrifice Taiwan's or Japan's defense preparedness on the altar of dubious "cooperation" with Beijing. If it does, it really ought to let Taipei (and Tokyo for that matter) know so they can start making separate plans—and they may be plans Washington will not like.

Military Support to Afghanistan and Arms Transfers to Pakistan Help the War on Terror

George W. Bush

George W. Bush is the forty-third president of the United States and was president at the time that this speech, from which the following is excerpted, was given.

Earlier this month [September 2006], our nation marked the fifth anniversary of the September 11th, 2001 terrorist attacks. We paused on that day to remember the innocent people who were killed that day. We paused to remember the rescue workers who rushed into burning towers to save lives. After 9/11, I stood in the well of the House of Representatives and declared that every nation, in every region, had a decision to make—either you were with us, or you stood with the terrorists. Two nations, Afghanistan and Pakistan, made very different decisions—with very different results.

Afghanistan After 9/11

Five years ago, Afghanistan was ruled by the brutal Taliban regime. Under the Taliban and al Qaeda, Afghanistan was a land where women were imprisoned in their own homes, where men were beaten for missing prayer meetings, where girls couldn't even go to school. What a hopeless society that was, under the rule of these hateful men. Afghanistan was the home to terrorist training camps. Under al Qaeda and the Taliban, Afghanistan was a terrorist safe haven and a launching pad for the horrific attacks that killed innocent people in New York City on September the 11th, 2001.

George W. Bush, "President Bush Discusses Global War on Terror," White House, September 29, 2006.

After 9/11, America gave the leaders of the Taliban a choice. We told them that they must turn over all the leaders of al Qaeda hiding in their land. We told them they must close every terrorist training camp and hand over every terrorist to appropriate authorities. We told them they must give the United States full access to the terrorist training camps, so they could make sure they were no longer operating. We told them these demands were not up for negotiation, and that if they did not comply immediately and hand over the terrorists, they would share in the same fate as the terrorists.

I felt these were reasonable demands. The Taliban regime chose unwisely—so within weeks after the 9/11 attacks, our coalition launched Operation Enduring Freedom. By December 2001, the Taliban regime had been removed from power, hundreds of Taliban and al Qaeda fighters had been captured or killed, and the terrorist camps where the enemy had planned the 9/11 attacks were shut down. We did what we said we were going to do. We made our intentions clear. We gave the Taliban a chance to make the right decision. They made the wrong decision, and we liberated Afghanistan.

---

*Our actions in Afghanistan have had a clear purpose . . .
and that is to rid that country of the Taliban and the
terrorists.*

The liberation of Afghanistan was a great achievement— and for those of you who served in that effort, thank you. I thank you on behalf of America, and the Afghan people thank you. But we knew that it was only the beginning of our mission in Afghanistan. See, the liberation was only the start of an important mission to make this world a more peaceful place. We learned the lesson of the 1980s, when the United States had helped the Afghan people drive the Soviet Red Army from Kabul, and then decided our work was finished, and left the Afghans to fend for themselves.

The Taliban came to power and provided a sanctuary for bin Laden and al Qaeda, and we paid the price when the terrorists struck our nation and killed nearly 3,000 people in our midst. So after liberating Afghanistan, we began the difficult work of helping the Afghan people rebuild their country, and establish a free nation on the rubble of the Taliban's tyranny. . . .

U.S. Military Support in Afghanistan

Our coalition is working with [Afghanistan] President Karzai to strengthen the institutions of Afghans—Afghanistan's young democracy. We understand that the institutions must be strengthened and reformed for democracy to survive. And one of the areas most in need of reform is the nation's legal system. Recently, President Karzai took important steps to strengthen the rule of law, when he appointed a new Attorney General and judges to serve on Afghanistan's Supreme Court. Our coalition is helping his government institutionalize these changes. Italy, for example, is helping to train Afghan judges, and prosecutors, and public defenders, and court administrators so all Afghans can receive equal justice under the law.

And from the beginning, our actions in Afghanistan have had a clear purpose—in other words, our goals are clear for people to understand—and that is to rid that country of the Taliban and the terrorists, and build a lasting free society that will be an ally in the war on terror. And from the beginning, the American people have heard the critics say we're failing—but their reasons keep changing. In the first days of Operation Enduring Freedom, the critics warned that we were heading toward a "quagmire." And then when the Taliban fell, and operations began in Iraq, the critics held up the multinational coalition in Afghanistan as a model, and said it showed that everything we were doing in Iraq was wrong. And now some of the critics who praised the multinational coalition we built in Afghanistan claim that the country is in danger of failing because we don't have enough American troops there.

Look, in order to win war, in order to win the ideological struggle of the 21st century, it is important for this country to have a clear strategy, and change tactics to meet the conditions on the ground, not try to constantly respond to the critics who change their positions. And so I listen to the advice of those who matter in Afghanistan, and that is President Karzai and our commanders. We will continue to help Afghanistan's government defeat our common enemies.

This ideological struggle of the 21st century will require tough military action.

Fighting the War on Terror Overseas

I've constantly told the American people we must defeat the enemy overseas, so we do not have to face them here at home. I will continue to remind the American people that you deal with threats before they materialize. In this war that we're in, it is too late to respond to a threat after the—after we've been attacked. I'm not going to forget the lessons of September the 11th, 2001, and I know you won't either. We must take threats seriously now, in order to protect the American people.

So we're going to help the people of Afghanistan, and help them build a free nation. We're going to help them be a successful part of defeating an ideology of hate with an ideology of hope. And think what that will mean for reformers and moderate people in a region that has been full of turmoil. Imagine the effect it will have when they see a thriving democracy in their midst.

No, this ideological struggle of the 21st century will require tough military action, good intelligence, it will require the United States to give our folks on the front line of terror the tools necessary to protect us, including listening to phone calls from al Qaeda coming into the country so we know what they're getting ready to attack or questioning people we capture on the battlefield. That's what it's going to include.

But it also means helping the millions who want to live in liberty to do so. In the long term, we will help our children and grandchildren live in a peaceful world by encouraging the spread of liberty.

Pakistan After 9/11

Five years ago, another country that faced a choice was Pakistan. At the time of 9/11, Pakistan was only one of three nations that recognized the Taliban regime in Afghanistan. Al Qaeda had a large presence in Pakistan. There was a strong radical Islamic movement in that country. Some of the 9/11 hijackers were housed and trained in Pakistan. Pakistan's future was in doubt—and President Musharraf understood that he had to make a fundamental choice for his people. He could turn a blind eye and leave the people hostage to the extremists, or he could join the free world in fighting the extremists and the terrorists. President Musharraf made the choice to fight for freedom, and the United States of America is grateful for his leadership.

Our close cooperation with the government of Pakistan has saved American lives.

Within two days of the September the 11th attacks, the Pakistani government committed itself to stop al Qaeda operatives at its border, to share intelligence on terrorist activities and movements, and to break off all ties with the Taliban government if it refused to hand over Bin Laden and the al Qaeda. President Musharraf's decision to fight the terrorists was made at great personal risk. They have tried to kill him as a result of his decision, because they know he has chosen to side with the forces of peace and moderation, and that he stands in the way of their hateful vision for his country.

President Musharraf's courageous choice to join the struggle against extremism has saved American lives. His government has helped capture or kill many senior terrorist leaders. For example, Pakistani forces helped capture Abu Zubaydah—a man we believe to be a trusted associate of Osama bin Laden. Pakistani forces helped capture another individual believed to be one of the key plotters of the 9/11 attacks—Ramzi bin al Shibh. Pakistani forces helped capture the man our intelligence community believes masterminded the 9/11 attacks—Khalid Sheikh Mohammed.

Once captured, these men were taken into custody of the Central Intelligence Agency. The questioning of these and other suspected terrorists provided information that helped us protect the American people. They helped us break up a cell of Southeast Asian terrorist operatives that had been groomed for attacks inside the United States. They helped us disrupt an al Qaeda operation to develop anthrax for terrorist attacks. They helped us stop a planned strike on a U.S. Marine camp in Djibouti [in eastern Africa], and to prevent a planned attack on the U.S. Consulate in Karachi [Pakistan], and to foil a plot to hijack passenger planes and to fly them into Heathrow Airport and London's Canary Wharf.

Were it not for the information gained from the terrorists captured with the help of Pakistan, our intelligence community believes that al Qaeda and its allies would have succeeded in launching another attack against the American homeland. Our close cooperation with the government of Pakistan has saved American lives—and America is grateful to have a strong and steadfast ally in the war against these terrorists.

U.S. Arms Support in Pakistan

President Musharraf understands that the terrorists hide in remote regions and travel back and forth across the border between Afghanistan and Pakistan. And so we're helping his government establish stronger control over these border areas. We are helping him to equip the nation's paramilitary Frontier Corps that is policing the border regions. The United States is funding the construction of more than 100 border outposts, which will provide Pakistani forces with better access to remote areas of the country's western border. We're providing high-tech equipment to help Pakistani forces better locate terrorists attempting to cross the border. We are funding an air wing with helicopters and fixed-wing aircraft to give Pakistan better security and surveillance capabilities.

And as we work with President Musharraf to bring security to his country, we're also supporting him as he takes steps to build a modern and moderate nation, that will hold free and fair elections next year. In an address to his fellow citizens earlier this year, President Musharraf declared this: "We have to eliminate extremism in our society. It will eat us up from within. So it is my appeal to all of you to shun extremism. Adopt the path of moderation . . . we will eliminate this extremism in our society and then Pakistan will be considered a moderate, developed country." President Musharraf has a clear vision for his country as a nation growing in freedom and prosperity and peace. And as he stands against the terrorists and for the free future of his country, the United States of America will stand with him.

The U.S. Must Work with Its Allies to Eliminate Terrorism

In both Pakistan and Afghanistan, America has strong allies who are committed to rooting out the terrorists in their midst. And with their help, we've killed or captured hundreds of al Qaeda leaders and operatives—and we put the others on the run. Osama bin Laden and other terrorists are still in hiding. Our message to them is clear: No matter how long it takes, we will find you, and we're going to bring you to justice.

On Wednesday night, I had dinner with Presidents Musharraf and Karzai at the White House. We had a long and we had a frank conversation about the challenges we face in defeating the extremists and the terrorists in their countries, and providing the people of these two nations an alternative to the dark ideology of the enemy. We discussed the best ways to improve intelligence sharing so that we can target and eliminate the leaders of al Qaeda and the Taliban.

We resolved to strengthen the institutions of civil society in both countries. We agreed on the need to support tribal leaders on both sides of the border. By helping these local leaders build schools, and roads, and health clinics, we will help them build a better life for their communities, and strengthen their hand against—to fight against the extremists. It was clear from our conversation that our three nations share the same goals: We will defeat the Taliban, we will defeat al Qaeda, and the only way to do it is by working together.

We're going to make it harder for them to recruit a new generation of terrorists.

The War on Terror Must Be Proactive

Our meeting took place at a time when there is a debate raging in Washington about how best to fight the war on terror. Recently, parts of a classified document called the National Intelligence Estimate [NIE] was leaked to the press. As I said yesterday in Alabama, it's an indication that we're getting close to an election. The NIE is a document that analyzes the threat we face from terrorists and extremists—and its unauthorized disclosure has set off a heated debate here in the United States, particularly in Washington.

Some have selectively quoted from this document to make the case that by fighting the terrorists, by fighting them in Iraq we are making our people less secure here at home. This argument buys into the enemy's propaganda that the terrorists attack us because we're provoking them. I want to remind the American citizens that we were not in Iraq on September the 11th, 2001.

And this argument was powerfully answered this week by [British] Prime Minister Tony Blair. Here is what he said. He said, "I believe passionately [that] we will not win until we shake ourselves free of the wretched capitulation to the propaganda of the enemy, that somehow we are the ones responsible." He went on to say, "This terrorism is not our fault. We didn't cause it. And it is not the consequence of foreign policy." He's right. You do not create terrorism by fighting terrorism. If that ever becomes the mind set of the policymakers in Washington, it means we'll go back to the old days of waiting to be attacked and then respond. Our most important duty is to protect the American people from a future attack, and the way to do so is to stay on the offense against the terrorists.

Iraq is not the reason the terrorists are at war against us. They are at war against us because they hate everything America stands for—and we stand for freedom. We stand for people to worship freely. One of the great things about America is, you're equally American if you're a Jew, a Muslim, a Christian, an agnostic or an atheist. What a powerful statement to the world about the compassion of the American people that you're free to choose the religion you want in our country. They can't stand the thought that people can go into the public square in America and express their differences with government. They can't stand the thought that the people get to decide the future of our country by voting. Freedom bothers them because their ideology is the opposite of liberty, it is the opposite of freedom. And they don't like it because we know they know we stand in their way of their ambitions in the Middle East, their ambitions to spread their hateful ideology as a caliphate [one united Muslim nation under Islamic law] from Spain to Indonesia.

We'll defeat the terrorists in Iraq. We'll deny them the safe haven to replace the one they lost in Afghanistan. We're going to make it harder for them to recruit a new generation of terrorists, and we're going to help the Iraqis build a free society. It's a hopeful country that sends a powerful message across the broader Middle East, and serves with those of us who believe in moderation and hope as an ally in the war against these extremists.

Current U.S. Arms Trade to Combat Terrorism Threatens Security

Rachel Stohl

Rachel Stohl is a senior analyst at the World Security Institute's Center for Defense Information (CDI) in Washington, D.C. She is coauthor of the book The Beginners Guide to the Small Arms Trade.

In November 2007, Pakistan's president, General Pervez Musharraf, invoked emergency rule, suspended the constitution, and arrested thousands of opponents and human rights advocates. As other countries, such as the Netherlands and Switzerland, immediately suspended military aid and weapons deals, the United States, which has given Pakistan more than $10 billion in military assistance since September 11, 2001, decided it would review U.S. arms transfers to Pakistan. Washington also indicated it would likely not prevent any weapons transfers, asserting such a decision could undermine counterterrorism efforts.

U.S. policy toward Pakistan is part of a larger trend of U.S. arms export policy since the September 11 attacks, whereby the United States has made the "global war on terror" its priority in determining arms transfers and military assistance. In the last six years, Washington has stepped up its sales and transfers of high-technology weapons, military training; and other military assistance to governments regardless of their respect for human rights, democratic principles, or nonproliferation. All that matters is that they have pledged their assistance in the global war on terrorism.

Rachel Stohl, "Questionable Reward: Arms Sales and the War on Terrorism," *Arms Control Today*, vol. 38, no. 1, January–February 2008, pp. 17–23. Copyright © 2008 Arms Control Association. Reproduced by permission.

U.S. Arms Sales and Export Policy Before and After September 11

To be sure, the United States traditionally has used arms sales to "reward" those countries willing to support its policies. The claimed motivations of such policies have changed over time from anti-communism to democracy building to anti-terrorism. The basic notion of using arms sales as a means of promoting loyalty to U.S. goals has been consistent.

Throughout this period, the United States has dominated the global arms market and continues to do so today. In 2006, Washington concluded the largest number of new arms deals ($16.9 billion worth in 2006, 41.9 percent of the global total) and made the most actual arms deliveries ($14 billion, nearly 52 percent of global arms deliveries). The United States' closest competitors were Russia and the United Kingdom, which made $8.7 billion and $3.1 billion in new deals, respectively, and delivered $5.8 billion and $3.3 billion worth of weapons. The United States has also regained its position atop exporters to the developing world, the largest purchasers of arms. Although the total global value of arms agreements fell in 2006, the United States saw multibillion-dollar increases in the value of its arms transfer agreements worldwide and with the developing world.

Nonetheless, there have been important changes since the September 11 attacks, with the United States finessing its arms export policies to support its war on terrorism. The most significant changes have involved the lifting of sanctions, the increase of arms and military training provided to perceived anti-terrorist allies, and the development of new programs focused and based on the global anti-terrorist crusade. To understand and document this trend, the Center for Defense Information has analyzed military assistance data (using U.S. government data solely) for 25 countries that have been identified by the United States as having a strategic role in the war on terrorism. These countries include those that reflect the counterterrorism priorities of the United States—17 are "front-line" states identified by the Bush administration as "countries that cooperate with the United States in the war on terrorism or face terrorist threats themselves"—and others strategically located near Afghanistan and Iraq.

U.S. transfers [of arms to previously sanctioned countries] could fuel ... human rights abuses by continuing conflict.

The U.S. Lifted Sanctions

Immediately after the attacks of September 11, the Bush administration proposed allowing arms sales to potential anti-terrorist allies that had previously been blocked from weapons transfers because they had committed significant human rights violations, lacked sufficient democratic institutions, had been involved in acts of aggression, or had tested nuclear weapons. Congressional opposition prevented these sanctions from being lifted *en bloc* [as a whole], and as a result, decisions to lift sanctions were made on a case-by-case basis. To date, the United States has completely lifted pre-September 11 sanctions on Armenia, Azerbaijan, India, Pakistan, Tajikistan, and the former Federal Republic of Yugoslavia (now Montenegro and Serbia). Since September 11, 2001, additional military assistance restrictions to Thailand and Indonesia have been waived.

These countries have been identified as key allies in the global war on terrorism, but each has troubling recent pasts, which led to them being placed on the list in the first place. Not only is each country involved in interstate or intrastate conflicts, but India and Pakistan have been criticized for their evolving nuclear weapons programs, Pakistan's and Thailand's military governments attained power as a result of coups, Azerbaijan has been embroiled for well more than a decade in a shaky ceasefire with Armenia, the stability of Tajikistan remains questionable, and the human rights record of Indonesia's military remains of great concern. Although sanctions have been removed, the conditions in these countries have not improved and in many cases have become worse. Nonetheless, arms transfers and other military assistance to all have increased. In addition, the human rights records of many of these countries have actually worsened, with increasing abuses by government and security forces. U.S. transfers could fuel these human rights abuses by continuing conflict. If the events of September 11, 2001, had never happened, these countries would likely still remain under strict U.S. sanctions.

The U.S. Increased Arms to Anti-Terrorism Allies

The second policy shift has been the Bush administration's commitment to using U.S. weapons to arm potential allies in the war against terrorism. On the six-month anniversary of the September 11 attacks, President George W. Bush declared that the United States was willing to provide training and assistance to any government facing a terrorist threat, stating that "America encourages and expects governments everywhere to help remove the terrorist parasites that threaten their own countries and peace of the world. If governments need training, or resources to meet this commitment, America will help."

In addition to the six countries that have had their sanctions lifted, the United States has provided military assistance to some countries that it had not aided previously in this way. For example, Yemen has received grants to acquire U.S weaponry for the last six years, but none in the 11 years prior to 2001. Turkmenistan is now buying U.S. weaponry, and Kyrgyzstan is now permitted to make commercial purchases of U.S. weapons. Even more telling, 18 of the 25 countries in this series received more military assistance and 16 concluded more arms sales with the United States during the five years after the September 11 attacks than they had during the period following the end of the Cold War (fiscal years 1990–2001).

Since September 11, 2001, the United States has offered military training to many countries that have experienced terrorism on their own soil.

In the first five years following September 11, 2001, the United States sold nearly five times more weapons through Foreign Military Sales (FMS) and Direct Commercial Sales (DCS) to these 25 countries than during the five years prior to that date. From fiscal year 2002 through fiscal year 2006, FMS to these countries increased from about $1.7 billion to $5.3 billion. DCS for these 25 countries have also reached new highs, rising from $72 million during fiscal years 1997–2001 to more than $3 billion during fiscal years 2002–2006. Pakistan had the largest increase in military sales (FMS and DCS) in the five-year period, signing agreements for $3.6 billion in U.S. defense articles. Other beneficiaries of the war on terrorism arms sale bonanza were Bahrain, which saw an increase of $1.6 billion, and Algeria, which saw an increase of nearly $600 million.

In Iraq, we have witnessed some of the drawbacks of this rush to arm and equip countries. In July 2007, the Government Accountability Office (GAO) released a report that revealed that nearly 200,000 weapons and other military equipment that the United States had provided to Iraqi security forces had not been accounted for. Among the weaknesses noted by the GAO was that the Department of Defense, which oversees the Iraqi train-and-equip program, neglected to implement basic accountability procedures to keep track of the distribution of weapons issued in 2004 and 2005. Today, the United States has not enunciated a clear plan to remedy these kinds of problems. Yet, as recently as September 2007, the top U.S. commander in Iraq, General David Petraeus, urged Washington to increase weapons sales to Iraq as soon as possible.

The U.S. Increased Training to Anti-Terrorism Allies

The United States has also viewed military training as an important aspect of its focus on fighting terrorism. A telling statement for the direction of U.S. policy was made in March 2002, when Bush emphasized U.S. reliance on training programs. He said, "We will not send American troops to every battle, but America will actively prepare other nations for the battles ahead." Since September 11, 2001, the United States has offered military training to many countries that have experienced terrorism on their own soil, are struggling with the presence of terrorist networks, or are essential to U.S. counterterrorism strategy.

In many cases, U.S. military assistance to these countries is growing at the same time as human rights conditions are worsening.

The overall funding for the International Military Education and Training (IMET) program has grown dramatically since 2001. For the 25 countries, the IMET program grew from $39 million in the five years prior to September 11, 2001, to $93 million in the five years after the attacks. That has also meant that the 25 countries are receiving an even greater percentage of total U.S. military training funds. In 2001 the 25 countries received 15 percent of total IMET funds, but by 2006, their share had jumped to nearly 25 percent.

Military Training Can Worsen the Situation

Although some of these countries are clearly involved with U.S. efforts to defeat al Qaeda and other terrorist networks, with others, such as those in Africa and Asia, the United States is gambling that military training will buy allies in the long run. Military training in many instances promotes the readiness, efficiency, and effectiveness of foreign military troops. It may also worsen the situation in countries plagued by terrorism if a well-armed and unaccountable military is not kept in check with human rights training and the country does not receive assistance building legal and judicial structures. Economic and social aid should also be offered concurrently to help strengthen and promote internal stability. Moreover, in some countries, such as Colombia, Nepal, and the Philippines, what is being described as counterterrorism training is in practice counterinsurgency training. The United States is involving itself in internal conflicts around the world and is in practice encouraging countries to continue their internal struggles that predate September 11, 2001. Not every insurgency is a threat to U.S. security, and some may in fact have very little to do with halting the spread of terrorism worldwide.

The Bush administration argues that professionalizing the world's militaries will help prevent human rights abuses down the road. Yet, the Department of State reveals in its annual human rights report that "serious," "grave," or "significant" abuses were committed by the government or state security forces in more than one-half of the 25 countries profiled in 2006 alone. In many cases, U.S. military assistance to these countries is growing at the same time as human rights conditions are worsening. Ethiopia, which is carrying out a brutal counterinsurgency campaign within its own borders, also launched an invasion of Somalia in December 2006 blamed for the deaths of scores of civilians and the displacement of at least 100,000 Somalis in indiscriminate violence in and around Mogadishu. Chad, which suffers from widespread turmoil and corruption, employs child soldiers in the ranks of its national army and is at a minimum tacitly involved in the ongoing regional conflicts in the Central African Republic and Sudan. By providing military assistance with a disregard for human rights conditions, the United States is not only giving up the opportunity to use military assistance as leverage to improve human rights conditions, but is also rewarding abusive governments for their unconscionable actions.

Moreover, in some of these countries, the military has contributed to domestic political turmoil and instability. In 2006 and 2007, Chad, Nepal, Pakistan, and Thailand dealt with pervasive and significant upheaval. Nepalese security forces opened fire on peaceful strikes and anti-government demonstrations. Chad's government barely survived a coup attempt. Thailand's government was taken over in a "peaceful" military coup. The Musharraf government's continuing battle against reform and political challengers led to the imposition of emergency rule, a move that abandons any pretense of democratic principles.

These sales are likely to mark only the beginning of U.S. military and defense industry ties with these questionable and challenging allies.

The U.S. Has Established New Programs

The third significant policy shift has been the creation of new Defense Department programs that provide training and weapons for counterterrorism operations outside traditional avenues of support. The Pentagon has long sought the freedom to provide military assistance without human rights conditions or other restrictions under current U.S. law as enunciated in the Foreign Assistance Act. In fiscal year 2002, the Regional Defense Counterterrorism Fellowship Program (CTFP) was created by Congress through the defense appropriations act with a mandate to provide nonlethal antiterrorism training. In fiscal year 2004, it began offering lethal training. In fiscal year 2006, Congress authorized the Defense Department to use $200 million of its operation and maintenance funds to equip and train foreign militaries for counter-terrorism operations, so-called Section 1206 authority.

Creating these parallel training authorities and funding them through the defense budget allows the Pentagon to bypass the Foreign Assistance Act and limits congressional oversight and the normally more cautious State Department from these decisions. In particular, it could help to sidestep restrictions on training or arming human rights abusers. For example, it could be argued that the CTFP essentially serves the same purpose as the State Department's IMET program but without any of the oversight or conditions.

The newly created Defense Department programs have provided training and equipment to all but four of the 25 countries examined. These programs come in addition to the aid provided through the five traditional major military assistance programs. For example, Yemen received more than $4 million in Section 1206 funding in fiscal year 2006 and an additional $200,000 in CTFP funding in fiscal year 2005, as well as $19.6 million in the five traditional types of aid in fiscal year 2006 and $14.6 million in such aid in fiscal year 2005.

Implications of Post-September 11 Policy Changes

Although the dollar value of the increased support for these countries could be seen as relatively insignificant compared to the considerably greater military assistance given to NATO [North Atlantic Treaty Organization] allies or countries in the Middle East, the relative shift from no or very few sales to millions or billions in military assistance in some cases matters greatly. After all, these sales are likely to mark only the beginning of U.S. military and defense industry ties with these questionable and challenging allies. The U.S. defense industry often relies on initial sales in order to encourage future sales; develop maintenance, consulting, or upgrades contracts; and set the stage for larger-ticket items down the road. Using the war on terrorism as their entrance card, these traditionally undesirable partners have gotten their feet in the door and will likely enjoy long-term military relationships with the United States. Indeed, for the most part, sales and training to these countries have grown every year. The United States must question whether these new allies and these transfers are consistent with long-standing principles and tenets of U.S. law.

Second, these transfers could pose significant risks to long-term U.S. security and stability. From the outset, much of this military assistance is inconsistent with U.S. efforts to spread peace and democracy throughout the world. Beyond the theoretical or principled contradiction, however, the reality is that once these weapons leave U.S. possession and training courses are completed, the United States cannot control how or by whom the weapons are used or the training is implemented. The situation in Iraq demonstrates this reality: U.S. weapons intended for Iraqi security forces have ended up in the hands of insurgents in Iraq and Turkey. In many cases, the countries receiving U.S. military assistance have only pledged assistance to the war on terrorism and may in fact behave in ways the United States opposes. Yet, little can be done in response beyond limiting future weapons and training.

Moreover, the United States suffers from the possibility of blowback—having these weapons used against U.S. troops, civilians, or interests down the road—a phenomenon the United States has experienced firsthand in Afghanistan and Iraq. Weapons provided to the mujahideen in the 1980s were used by the Taliban and today's Afghan rebels. In Iraq, weapons provided to Saddam Hussein during the 1980s remain in circulation and in the hands of Iraqi insurgents. The Bush administration's policy of arming these new allies for short-term gains could put the United States at considerable risk and result in the United States facing its own weapons as political alliances deteriorate. Because the United States has increased transfers and training to countries that have dismal records on democracy, human rights, and loyalty, it is not too far a stretch to believe that some of these new allies could turn against the United States in the future.

The track records of many of these recipients—poor human rights records, prior support for and harboring of terrorists, or consistently undemocratic regimes—have been ignored by the Bush administration in an effort to bolster the war on terrorism. In doing so, the United States loses the ability to encourage a change in these bad actors' behavior and does not guarantee that these short-term allies will remain long-term U.S. partners. Furthermore, the instability in many of these countries also raises questions about their future allegiance.

The United States should look at other ways of cooperating with new allies.

Ironically, the provision of weapons, aid, and training to some states might even ultimately serve to undermine the U.S. goal of eradicating terrorism. Countries benefiting from new access to weapons and training may see the continuation of the war on terrorism to be in their own best interest. They may not seriously commit to fighting terrorism because an end to terrorist threats, either real or perceived, might mean a decrease in aid. Thus, the actual dedication of many of these countries to U.S. goals and policies may leave much to be desired.

An Alternative to Current U.S. Policy

Rather than continuing its current approach, the United States would be better served by abiding by its long-standing arms export laws to ensure that weapons exports do not undermine security and stability, weaken democracy, support military coups, escalate arms races, exacerbate ongoing conflicts, or cause arms buildups in unstable regions or are used to commit human rights abuses. Although the war on terrorism has taken center stage, these principles and values should not be given an end run. This may mean that even close allies, such as Djibouti, Ethiopia, and Pakistan, which have worsening or no improvement in their human rights records, have their military assistance scaled back until substantial improvements are made. The United States should look at other ways of cooperating with new allies, such as economic and development assistance, and work to strengthen these partners' democracies and institutions. More than ever, the United States needs strong partners that value human rights and the rule of law.

If arms and training are the only foreign policy tools the United States is willing to use, then they must be provided in line with U.S. law and under the strictest oversight and accountability. Programs should not be allowed to bypass U.S. law. New Defense Department programs should be scaled back and evaluated, rather than expanded, to ensure that they are upholding U.S. law. If the United States does sell weapons and provide training to questionable new allies, all effort should be taken to ensure that these weapons do not undermine U.S. security down the road.

The Arms Trade to the Middle East Leads to Greater Instability

William D. Hartung

William D. Hartung is director of the arms and security initiative at the New America Foundation, a nonprofit, nonpartisan public policy institute. He is an expert on the arms trade and military spending, and the author of And Weapons for All.

Under the guise of promoting a "security dialogue" in the Persian Gulf, the Bush Administration has proposed $63 billion in arms transfers to the Middle East over the next ten years. As is so often the case, team Bush seems to prefer to let the weapons do the talking, even when it claims to be engaging in diplomacy. The foundation of the deal is a pledge to sell $20 billion worth of high-tech arms to Saudi Arabia and the other oil-producing states in the Gulf. Items in the package reportedly include upgrades to Riyadh's US-supplied fighter planes, satellite-guided bombs and combat ships. To ease any concerns about the Gulf buildup, the plan calls for increasing military aid to Israel and Egypt to $3 billion and $1.3 billion per year, respectively. That's $43 billion in US taxpayer support over the next decade.

The Rationale for Middle East Arms Transfers Is Flawed

Why pour more weapons into the region now? The principal rationale appears to be to send a message to Iran that it must bend to US pressure to end its nuclear program, stop the flow of Iranian weapons to Iraqi insurgents and cease its support for Hamas and Hezbollah. Otherwise, the argument goes, not only will Tehran face the prospect of US military action but it will also be surrounded by neighbors armed with top-of-the-line US weaponry. The arms package will be seen as even more provocative by Iran in light of the latest move in the Bush Administration's campaign to turn up the pressure on the regime: the recent decision to label its Islamic Revolutionary Guard Corps a terrorist organization.

Threatening Iran with military strikes and arms sales to potential adversaries is more likely to spur Tehran to add to its own arsenal while being less open to talks on its nuclear program. If the Bush Administration is looking for a new designated enemy to stand in for the late Saddam Hussein, this approach will work just fine. But if it wants to solve the security problems of the region, it would be hard to come up with a more counterproductive policy.

Saudi Arabia, Egypt, and Israel Should Not Receive U.S. Arms

Secretary of State Condoleezza Rice and Secretary of Defense Robert Gates have tried to paper over the real intent of the deal by arguing that it will promote "stability" by bolstering moderate regimes. This is a strange assertion, especially as regards Saudi Arabia. Not only are funds from Saudi sources supporting insurgents in Iraq, but they are financing Islamic extremism around the world. The Saudis also operate one of the most repressive regimes on the planet, in direct contradiction of the Administration's continuing claims to be promoting democracy. The State Department's latest human rights report on Saudi Arabia contains this upbeat passage: "Religious police harassed, abused and detained citizens and foreigners of both sexes." The most recent Human Rights Watch Saudi report points out that "the government undertook no major human rights reforms in 2006, and there were signs of backsliding in issues of human rights defenders, freedom of association, and freedom of expression." Sending more weapons will not reverse these trends, which does not bode well for long-term stability in the Saudi kingdom.

In Egypt, decades of US aid have had no positive impact on human rights or democracy. Egyptian President Hosni Mubarak runs a quasi-Stalinist regime that won 88 percent of the vote in the last national elections while jailing numerous democracy advocates. As the State Department has acknowledged, torture is still widely practiced in Egyptian prisons, while Cairo's overall human rights record is described as "poor." Rewarding the Egyptian government with an increase in US military aid is tantamount to condoning these repressive practices—practices that are producing a popular backlash that could eventually lead to the end of the regime. If that happens, whatever government comes to power next will inherit huge stockpiles of US-supplied weaponry.

As for Israel, more military aid is the last thing it needs. In recent times Tel Aviv has used its military in ways that have undermined its own security as well as that of its neighbors. From the ongoing attacks on Gaza to last summer's invasion of Lebanon, the Israeli government has unintentionally offered aid and comfort to hard-line forces, both among the Palestinians and in Lebanon. Israel has plenty of weapons; what it needs is a return to genuine diplomacy, ideally prodded by its closest ally, Washington.

Only Arms Makers Will Benefit

Sixty years of arms racing has repeatedly undermined prospects for Middle East peace. Why should this latest round be any different? The only clear beneficiaries of this mega-deal will be US arms makers. Already gorging on expenditures for the wars in Iraq and Afghanistan, companies like Boeing, General Electric and General Dynamics can anticipate ten years of lucrative foreign sales if the deal goes forward. . . .

Mideast stability can't be promoted with arms, any more than democracy can be imposed through the barrel of a gun. Stopping or scaling back the Bush Administration's Mideast arms package would be a step toward learning this lesson.

Arms Trade with Taiwan Could Cause a World War

Craig Crawford

Craig Crawford is a news analyst for NBC, MSNBC, and CNBC. He is also a contributing editor for CQ Weekly, *where the following viewpoint was originally published.*

I routinely read polls after dousing them in a full heaping of salt, but a recent Associated Press survey gave me disturbing pause: 60 percent of Americans expect to endure World War III in their lifetimes.

Indeed, such a lopsided answer to such a frightening question is worth more than a pause. It should be the main issue in the nation's coming elections—not only in next year's [2006] midterm battle for control of Congress, but also in the 2008 race for the White House.

The questions voters would use to frame their choices are simple: Which candidates or parties have the best plan to avoid the sort of global catastrophe that three out of five Americans expect they'll witness? In electing the 110th Congress and the 44th president, is it preferable to seek continuity with the Big Planners of the Bush war team, or would it be better to make an entirely new set of plans for avoiding World War III?

Sadly, there is little guidance for answering such questions now, for they are not even on the table as politicians bicker back and forth about homeland security, troop levels in Iraq and what to do about North Korea.

Washington Insiders Believe War with China Is Inevitable

The AP poll (1,000 Americans were interviewed between July 5–10, and the results have a 3 percentage point margin of sampling error) brought to mind a startling dinner I had several years ago with some very powerful men who spent hours discussing, with alarming certainty, the likelihood of war with China in our lifetimes.

Long before the Sept. 11 attacks intensified the nation's necessary obsession with Islamic terrorists, I had been invited by the publisher of an influential magazine to dinner at his Washington mansion with a former director of the CIA, a top executive of one of the nation's largest defense contractors, and a former congressman-turned-lobbyist. I sat slack-jawed as these authoritative sources matter-of-factly analyzed U.S. strategies for defeating China. Most remarkable was their unanimous view that such a war is inevitable—that the only debatable question was how to win it.

This new administration was not shy about saber-rattling with China.

I don't recall much about the military scenarios, including the horrific estimates of U.S. casualties, because in return for the invitation I agreed never to report such details. So my main memory is of leaving with the unsettlingly distinct impression that the Big Planners of Washington were seriously gunning for a war that could provoke a worldwide calamity. Many more dinners like this, I thought, and I might have to join a self-sufficiency cult in Idaho.

U.S. Policy with Taiwan Could Cause Problems with China

The last time that evening came to mind with such urgency was when I was listening to an interview that ABC's Charlie

Gibson had with George W. Bush in April 2001. In it, the new president defended his backing of the largest U.S. arms sale to Taiwan in history by seemingly issuing the most specific military threat to China of any recent president. He vowed to respond "with the full force of American military" if China ever attacked Taiwan, saying he would do "whatever it took to help Taiwan defend herself."

There was much hullabaloo at the time about this apparently new—and more strident—policy toward China, accompanied by the usual White House guidance, on background, that the president didn't really mean to change what had been the longstanding and intentional vagueness of our commitment to defend Taiwan. But there was no mistaking that this new administration was not shy about saber-rattling with China, especially in the wake of the collision of a U.S. spy plane and a Chinese jet earlier that month. Five months later, terrorists struck on U.S. soil, and China was all but forgotten, as war in Afghanistan and Iraq consumed the world's attention.

Now there is reason to wonder if Bush's Big Planners are ready to return to the saber-rattling of their pre-Sept. 11 stance against China. Secretary of Defense Donald H. Rumsfeld recently touted a new Pentagon assessment of China's military power, noting that its defense spending is much higher than Chinese officials have reported publicly and that China is expanding its missile forces "allowing it to reach targets in many areas of the world."

The Air Force's top military officer, Gen. Michael Moseley, said at his Senate confirmation hearing in June that lining up American firepower for a possible war with China is "at the top of my list."

But it was a Chinese military leader, the hawkish Major General Zhu Chenghu, who really stoked the embers recently when he seemed to answer Bush's 2001 threat by saying China would "respond with nuclear weapons" in a conflict over Taiwan. "If the Americans are determined to interfere, then we will be determined to respond," he said. "The Americans will have to be prepared that hundreds of cities will be destroyed by the Chinese."

Such incendiary talk justifies the public's fear of a world war. It is hard to imagine anything more crucial for public debate in the elections ahead.

Arms Trade with Pakistan and India Does Not Improve U.S. Relations

Zia Mian

Zia Mian is a physicist with the Program on Science and Global Security at the Woodrow Wilson School of Public and International Affairs at Princeton University and a columnist for Foreign Policy In Focus, a nonprofit think tank and Web site that publishes the research of scholars, advocates, and activists in order to make the United States an informed and responsible world partner.

The United States sells death, destruction, and terror as a fundamental instrument of its foreign policy. It sees arms sales as a way of making and keeping strategic friends and tying countries more directly to U.S. military planning and operations. At its simplest, as Lt. Gen. Jeffrey B. Kohler, director of the Defense Security Cooperation Agency, told the *New York Times* in 2006, the United States likes arms deals because "it gives us access and influence and builds friendships." South Asia has been an important arena for this effort, and it teaches some lessons the United States should not ignore.

The Scale of U.S. Arms Sales

A recent Congressional Research Service report on international arms sales records that last year the United States delivered nearly $8 billion worth of weapons to Third World countries. This was about 40% of all such arms transfers. The United States signed agreements to sell over $10 billion worth of weapons, one-third of all arms deals with Third World countries.

It is easy to put this in perspective: $10 billon a year is the estimated cost of meeting the UN Millennium Development Goal for water and sanitation, which would reduce by half the proportion of people in the world without proper access to drinking water and basic sanitation by 2015. Today, about 1.1 billion people do not have access to a minimal amount of clean water and about 2.6 billion people do not have access to basic sanitation.

The scale of recent U.S. arms sales should not be news. The United States sold over $61 billion worth of weapons to Third World countries from 1999–2006, making it by far the leading international supplier. Russia, the second largest arms dealer, managed to sell less than half as much.

Arms Versus Influence in Pakistan

The largest third world buyer of weapons in 2006 was Pakistan. It purchased just over $5 billion in arms deals. Almost $3 billion of the purchases by Pakistan were new U.S.-made F-16 fighter jets, up-grades to the F-16s Pakistan bought in the 1980s, and bombs and missiles to arm these planes. A White House Press spokesman explained that the sale of the jet fighters "demonstrates our commitment to a long-term relationship with Pakistan."

The use of arms sales to show commitment to Pakistan has gone on for over 50 years. The United States used military aid to recruit and arm Pakistan as an ally in the Cold War. A great fear, as a 1953 State Department memorandum pointed out, was "a noticeable increase in the activities of the mullahs in Pakistan. There was reason to believe that in face of growing doubts as to whether Pakistan had any real friends, more and more Pakistanis were turning to the mullahs for guidance. Were this trend to continue the present government of enlightened and Western-oriented leaders might well be threatened, and members of a successive government would probably be far less cooperative with the west than the present incumbents." This memo could have been written today.

The United States has failed to learn that paying Pakistan's military bills demonstrates commitment and friendship only to Pakistan's army. It does nothing for Pakistan's people. The US supported General Ayub Khan, Pakistan's first military leader, for a decade (1958–1969), at great cost. He was brought down by a tide of public protest.

There is little doubt today about how unpopular the United States is in Pakistan.

The United States also supported General Zia (who ruled from 1977 to 1988), once he agreed to help in the U.S. war against the Soviet Union occupation in Afghanistan. Washington gave General Zia a $3.2 billion aid package in 1982 and promised another $4 billion in 1988. This generosity bought precious little. Pakistan's government took the money and used it to buy weapons from the United States, built nuclear weapons, and promoted radical Islamists at home and in Afghanistan. The consequences are all around us today.

Since September 11, 2001, the United States has given over $10 billion to Pakistan to buy or reward General Musharraf's support for its newest war, the "war on terror." Pakistan has spent over $1.5 billion of this amount on buying new weapons. To understand the scale of this aid, consider Pakistan's total military budget in 2006, estimated at about $4.5 billion. The United States is now giving Pakistan aid to pay for the new deal for F-16s, bombs, and missiles. It is likely to win few friends.

There is little doubt today about how unpopular the United States is in Pakistan. A Pew Poll released in September 2006 found that in Pakistan, the United States is viewed less favorably even than India (with which Pakistan has fought four wars). Just over 25% were favorable toward the United States, compared to one-third who felt that way toward India.

India, Pakistan's neighbor, historic rival, and often bitter enemy, is the second largest buyer of weapons in the Third World.

Attitudes toward the United States have worsened. A 2007 poll found that only 15% of Pakistanis had a favorable attitude towards the United States. An August 2007 poll found that General Musharraf was less popular even than Osama bin Laden; Musharraf had the support of 38% of Pakistanis, Bin Laden of 46%, and President Bush found favor with only 9%. It is hard to imagine a more damning indictment of a policy that sought to make friends and build support.

This hostility toward the United States will only get worse as it is seen to support General Musharraf's efforts to remain president of Pakistan.

U.S. Attempt at a Strategic Relationship with India

India, Pakistan's neighbor, historic rival, and often bitter enemy, is the second largest buyer of weapons in the Third World. It signed up for $3.5 billion worth of weapons in 2006. It is now responsible for about 12% all arms purchases in the third world. India has traditionally bought Russian weapons, but is now interested in what others, especially the United States, has to offer.

India may spend some $40 billion on weapons purchases over the next five years. High on the list is a contract for 126 jet fighters, with a possible price tag of over $10 billion. A State Department official announced the government will try to help win the order for a U.S. company. U.S. arms manufacturers are already lining up. Richard G. Kirkland, Lockheed Martin's president for South Asia, has claimed that "India is our top market" when it come to "potential for growth." The President of Raytheon Asia, Waiter F. Doran, claims India may be "one of our largest, if not our largest, growth partner over the next decade or so."

There is good reason for U.S. confidence. In 2005, the defense secretaries of the United States and India signed the "New Framework for the U.S.-India Defense Relationship." The Framework "charts a course for the U.S.-India defense relationship for the next ten years" and "will support, and will be an element of, the broader U.S.-India strategic partnership." It includes a commitment to "expand two-way defense trade." These arms deals, the Framework statement claims, should be seen "not solely as ends in and of themselves, but as a means to strengthen our countries' security, reinforce our strategic partnership, achieve greater interaction between our armed forces, and build greater understanding between our defense establishments."

More Arms, Less Influence

As with Pakistan, these arms sales may not buy the United States the influence it seeks in India. The U.S.-India nuclear deal offers an example of how things may play out. In 2005, the United States and India agreed on a deal to exempt India from the 30-year-old U.S. laws that prevent states from using commercial imports of nuclear technology and fuel to aid their nuclear weapons ambitions. In 2006, Congress approved and President Bush signed legislation lifting the curbs on nuclear trade with India. The two countries have been negotiating a nuclear cooperation agreement over the past year.

The clearest exposition of what the United States wants in exchange came in testimony to Congress in support of the U.S.-India nuclear deal by Ashton Carter, who served as assistant secretary of defense in the Clinton administration, and in a 2006 article "America's New Strategic Partner?" in the journal *Foreign Affairs*. He argued that Washington needed India's help against Iranian nukes, in future conflicts with Pakistan, and as a counterweight to China. He noted there were "more direct benefits," which include "the intensification of military-to-military contacts" and "the cooperation of India in disaster-relief efforts, humanitarian interventions, peacekeeping missions, and post-conflict reconstruction efforts," and "operations not mandated by or commanded by the United Nations, operations in which India has historically refused to participate."

And finally, Carter offered the real kicker, "U.S. military forces may also seek access to strategic locations through Indian territory and perhaps basing rights there. Ultimately, India could even provide U.S. forces with 'over-the-horizon' bases for contingencies in the Middle East."

Carter recognized that there are other interests too, which others might put higher on the list. He acknowledged that "on the economic front, as India expands its civilian nuclear capacity and modernizes its military, the United States stands to gain preferential treatment for U.S. industries."

The process of putting pressure on India to deliver has already begun. In May 2007, key members of the U.S. Congress wrote a letter to the Indian prime minister warning that they were "deeply concerned" by India's relationship with Iran, and that if India did not address this then there was "the potential to seriously harm prospects for the establishment of the global partnership between the United States and India." In short, India was being told to choose: Iran or the United States and the nuclear deal.

However, the past few weeks [September 2007] have seen a growing crisis in India over the nuclear deal and how close India should get to the United States. India's Communist Parties, which are part of the Congress Party-led coalition government, have demanded a halt to the U.S.-India nuclear deal to give the country time to work out its implications for Indian foreign policy. Their fear is that the deal will give the

U.S. influence over Indian decision-making. They have threatened to bring down India's government.

India's progressive social movements have also opposed the nuclear deal. They worry that "directly or indirectly, the United States will also enter the Indian sub-continent, to manage intra-regional, inter-country relations." They see it as "not just anti-democratic but against peace, and against environmentally sustainable energy generation and self-reliant economic development." These basic concerns about democracy, peace, sustainability, and independence, are what will put India at odds with U.S. policy, no matter how many weapons it offers to sell.

CHAPTER 3

Does the Arms Trade Need More Global Regulation?

Chapter Preface

The question of the need for global regulation of the arms trade tends to elicit different answers depending on what kinds of arms are in question. Arms can be divided into two main categories: weapons of mass destruction and conventional weapons. Weapons of mass destruction, including chemical, biological, and nuclear weapons, can kill large numbers of people, cause extreme damage to natural and man-made structures, or cause extreme damage to the environment. Examples of weapons of mass destruction include nuclear bombs, nerve agents such as sarin, and organisms such as anthrax. Conventional weapons include guns, tanks, and land mines.

Arms regulation, both regional and global, generally has been more accepted with respect to weapons of mass destruction. The Outer Space Treaty bars weapons of mass destruction in outer space; the Nuclear Non-Proliferation Treaty limits the proliferation of nuclear weapons by setting limits on the acquisition, trade, and use of nuclear technology; and the Biological and Toxin Weapons Convention, along with the Chemical Weapons Convention, supplement the Geneva Protocol of 1925, banning the use of biological and chemical weapons. However, the effectiveness of these agreements regarding weapons of mass destruction is limited, because some countries are not parties to the agreements.

Regulation of conventional weapons is spottier on an international level. Many countries have national laws regulating the possession, trade, and production of conventional weapons, but international regulations or agreements are rare. Certain exceptions include the Ottawa Treaty, which bans the production, transfer, and use of anti-personnel (used against humans) mines, and the Convention on Certain Conventional Weapons, which prohibits or limits the use of certain weapons and munitions, including fragmentation weapons, landmines, certain inflammatory devices, and blinding laser weapons, considered to have inhumane effects. As with the treaties and conventions that control the use of weapons of mass destruction, not all countries have joined these two international agreements on the use of conventional weapons, which, again, limits the effectiveness of the agreements.

Regional agreements have been voluntarily joined by countries in certain regions to control the transfer of arms. Such agreements include the Central American (SICA) Code of Conduct on Arms Transfers (2006), the West African (ECOWAS) Convention on Small Arms and Light Weapons (2006), and the Best Practice Guidelines for the Nairobi Protocol on Small Arms (2005). Nonetheless, none of these commitments is legally binding and, without ratification by all countries globally, arms transfers banned in one place can occur elsewhere.

Many have argued that the arms trade needs more global controls. Persuading individual countries to agree to treaties regarding weapons of mass destruction has been somewhat successful. But even with respect to nuclear weapons, worldwide agreement has not been forthcoming: Israel, India, and Pakistan are not signatories to the Nuclear Non-Proliferation Treaty, and North Korea withdrew from the treaty in 2003. The United Nations has taken steps toward a global Arms Trade Treaty, but because of concerns about how it would affect rights to gun ownership, among other things, the United States voted against one of the first proposals for such a treaty. Because the opinions of individual nations diverge so greatly on the issues of whether global arms trade control is needed and exactly what kind of control is preferable, it remains to be seen whether or not global controls for the arms trade are a possibility.

Global Controls Are Needed for the Arms Trade

Edmund Cairns

Edmund Cairns is research coordinator of Oxfam International's humanitarian campaign. Oxfam International is a global organization that works to fight poverty.

If the current growth in worldwide military spending continues, by the end of 2006 it will have passed the highest figure reached during the Cold War. After year-on-year increases since 1999, global military spending this year is estimated to reach an unprecedented $1,058.9bn [billion], which is roughly 15 times annual international aid expenditure. This is not due to the growth in arms sales alone; military spending covers other costs beside. But in 2005, estimated global spending on arms alone was 34 per cent higher than in 1996. The post-Cold War decline is long gone.

The Increase in Global Military Spending

Global military spending is increasing and expanding the market for the global arms trade. This growth shows no signs of reversal as its key drivers—the 'war on terror', the conflicts in Iraq, Afghanistan and the Middle East among others, and the increased military spending by large, fast-growing countries—seem set to continue.

Some of the increased military spending is in countries least able to afford it. Some of the poorest countries in the world, including Botswana, the Democratic Republic of

Edmund Cairns, *Arms without Borders: Why a Globalised Trade Needs Global Controls.* London, U.K.: Amnesty International, The International Action Network on Small Arms, and Oxfam, 2006. Copyright © 2006 Amnesty International Publications, 1 Easton Street, London WC1X 0DW, U.K., The International Action Network on Small Arms, and Oxfam International. Reproduced with the permission of Oxfam GB, Oxfam House, John Smith Drive, Cowley, Oxford OX4 2Jy U.K., www.oxfam.org.uk, and Amnesty International, www.amnesty.org. Oxfam GB does not necessarily endorse any text or activities that accompany the materials, nor has it approved the adapted text.

Congo, Nigeria, Rwanda, Sudan and Uganda, are among those that doubled their military spending between 1985 and 2000. In 2002–03, Bangladesh, Nepal and Pakistan were among those governments that spent more on their military than on health-care.

In some developing countries, high military spending bears little relation to real defence needs. In Angola, for example, the proportion of GDP [Gross Domestic Product] devoted to military spending more than doubled in the two years *after* its 27-year-long war ended in 2002, rising to 4.2 per cent.

Part of this increase in military spending is the growth in arms sales in the developing world. In 2004, the US Congressional Research Service estimated that collectively, countries in Asia, the Middle East, Latin America and Africa spent $22.5bn on arms, 8 per cent more than they did in 2003 (where figures are estimated at $20.8bn). This sum would have enabled those countries to put every child in school and to reduce child mortality by two-thirds by 2015 (fulfilling two of the Millennium Development Goals).

The arms trade is not just larger, but now more 'globalised' than ever before.

The Growth of the International Arms Trade

Overall, the international trade in arms, having shrunk in the 1990s, has been growing in parallel with the growth in total military spending. Between 2000 and 2004, the approximate value of arms exports increased from $35.6bn to $53.3bn in constant 2003 prices. This does not include most of the fast-growing trade in weapons components.

Between 2000 and 2004, the top 100 companies reportedly increased their domestic and international sales of conventional weapons from $157bn to $268bn, an increase of nearly

60 per cent. Excluding China, for whose companies there is insufficient data, 85 of the world's top 100 arms companies in 2003 were headquartered in the industrialised world. The USA-based Boeing and Lockheed Martin topped the list with arms sales of $27.5bn and $26.4bn respectively.

The Globalisation of the Arms Trade

The arms trade is not just larger, but now more 'globalised' than ever before, as a result of the continuing and cumulative transformation of the industry since at least the early 1990s.

The top 100 arms companies no longer simply build weapons. They integrate components made all over the world. Analysing the global spread of arms and military power, one account of globalisation stated in 1999 that 'in few other domains has globalisation been so extensive, visibly encompassing the globe, or . . . so (potentially) catastrophic' [as quoted in D. Held et al. 1999].

Like products in most other industries, very few pieces of military equipment are now manufactured entirely in one country. Instead, components are sourced from across the globe, production facilities are set up in new, often developing, countries, brokers and dealers flourish, technology is traded, and arms companies produce their branded weapons in many locations.

When major Western arms companies co-operate with partners in other countries they can develop and penetrate new markets, while their partners can gain access to cutting-edge technology. In the Middle Ages, it took two centuries for cutting-edge arms technology (gunpowder) to be transferred across the world, from China to Europe. In the twenty-first century, it is very much quicker. . . .

Emerging Arms-Exporting Countries

The emerging arms-exporting countries are still a small part of the total industry compared with the five states that have traditionally dominated the arms trade for years—the USA, Russia, the UK, France and Germany. These five together accounted for an estimated 82 per cent of all major conventional arms transfers in 2005. However, exporters such as Brazil, China, India, Israel, Pakistan, Singapore, South Korea, South Africa and Turkey are playing an increasing role in the global arms trade. Other countries such as Jordan and Malaysia are actively developing their defence industries and export potential.

The transfer of technology and sophisticated arms production capacity is increasing.

The number of arms companies in the top 100 that are based in countries not previously considered as major exporters has more than doubled since 1990. Brazil, India, Israel, Singapore, South Africa and South Korea now all have companies in the world's top 100. Several Chinese companies would also probably figure in the top 100 had they been included in the survey. Among all these countries, national arms export controls vary, and do not always include explicit criteria or guidelines for authorising arms transfers that fully reflect states' existing obligations under international law.

Much of these countries' production is geared for export. For example, despite Israel's substantial domestic defence market, two-thirds of its arms output is reportedly destined for foreign buyers. Its four arms companies in the top 100—Israel Aircraft Industries, Elbit, Rafael, and Israel Military Industries—must look abroad for much of their profits.

The Arms Produced by Emerging Exporters

The transfer of technology and sophisticated arms production capacity is increasing. The Eurocopter Group, a subsidiary of EADS (European Aeronautic, Defence and Space Company) claims to be the world's top helicopter manufacturer with 16 subsidiaries on five continents and more than 2,500 customers in 139 countries. Eurocopter has played a key role in the transfer of technology and production capacity to four countries—China, India, South Africa and South Korea—all recent entrants to the armed or attack helicopters market.

At the other end of the technology spectrum, there are some 92 countries producing small arms and light weapons. At least 14 countries make the ubiquitous Kalashnikov assault rifle, including, for example, Egypt and North Korea. In June 2006, the *Financial Times* revealed that Russia had supplied 30,000 Kalashnikov weapons to Venezuela as part of a $54m deal that would also allow Venezuela to become the first Western hemisphere producer of the world's best-selling rifle.

Similarly, there are now 76 countries which manufacture small arms ammunition, and the number is growing. In May 2006, a survey in Baghdad's black market found ammunition that had been made in factories in seven different countries: Bulgaria, China, the Czech Republic, Hungary, Romania, Russia, and Serbia. In 1998 it was reported that a plant in Eldoret in Kenya produced an estimated 20 million rounds of ammunition per year, after importing production equipment from Belgium in the late 1990s.

One indication of increasing globalisation in the arms industry can be seen in company participation at international defence exhibitions. Researchers for the Control Arms campaign have analysed participation at several international arms fairs over recent years. At Eurosatory 1992, a defence exhibition held in Paris, there were only two companies exhibiting from outside Europe and both were from the Middle East. At Eurosatory 2006 the picture was radically different, with 52 companies exhibiting from the Middle East and ten companies from the Asia Pacific region. At IDEX, an annual defence exhibition held in the United Arab Emirates, a similar pattern is evident. Between 1999 and 2006 participation from companies from Asia Pacific more than doubled, and for South-East

Asia the increase was threefold. At DSA 2006, an annual exhibition held in Malaysia, there was a significant increase in companies from India, Malaysia, South Korea and Turkey as compared to previous years. . . .

Some companies and new exporting nations are seeking their competitive edge based in part upon their lack of strict export controls.

The Arms Industry and Lack of Controls

National and regional arms control agreements are necessary elements of an effective system for stopping transfers which contribute to unnecessary human suffering. But there are many ways around them. . . .

The major global arms companies are driven by a range of economic motives: to lower costs, find new markets and share the expense of developing new products. But whatever their motive, their global out-sourcing, licensed production and joint ventures all make it more difficult for governments to control the supply of arms around the world.

At the same time, some companies and new exporting nations are seeking their competitive edge based in part upon their lack of strict export controls. They will be able to sell in 'dirty' markets that other governments would not allow. Jordan's national strategy to expand its Defense-Scientific Industrial Base sets out its mission in these terms: 'to ensure that core technologies and products can be manufactured, marketed and supplied without being subject to external export and licensing controls' [as quoted in *Jane's International Defence Review*, October 1, 2002].

Arms Control Initiatives Around the World

Nevertheless, the same years that have witnessed this expansion in the global arms industry have also seen a number of initiatives to improve the control of arms exports, though most involve non-legally binding instruments.

In 1993, the OSCE (Organisation for Security and Co-operation in Europe) agreed Criteria on Conventional Arms Transfers that require governments to avoid exports likely to be used for human rights violations. Then in 1996, the most powerful multilateral group of arms-supplier countries, the 39 governments of the Wassenaar Arrangement, agreed the 'Initial Elements' of an arms control and information exchange regime. This was subsequently amended to produce the 'Purposes, Guidelines and Procedures, including Initial Elements' currently adopted by the participating states, including 'Best Practice Guidelines for Exports of Small Arms and Light Weapons' agreed in 2002, which also include a requirement to avoid exports likely to be used for human rights violations. However, of the new exporters listed . . . only South Africa is a participant.

In 1998, the European Union, led by the UK and France, agreed a Code of Conduct on Arms Transfers, again with a stipulation to not export arms where there is a 'clear risk' of internal repression or external aggression. In the same year the governments of Southern Africa agreed to strengthen their controls on arms transfers as part of a wider Regional Action Programme on Light Arms, part of the process which led to the Southern African Development Community (SADC) Protocol on the Control of Firearms, Ammunition and other Related Materials in 2001. However, the Protocol did not incorporate standards from international human rights or humanitarian law.

In 1999, 20 governments in the Organisation of American States agreed an Inter-American Convention on transparency in buying conventional weapons.

In 2004, the governments of the Horn and East Africa agreed a Nairobi Protocol, consisting of criteria intended to govern the transfer of small arms around their war-torn region. The 'best practice guidelines' agreed in 2005 for this Protocol contain detailed provisions relating to the need to protect international human rights and humanitarian law as well as sustainable development.

In 2005, the seven governments of the Sistema de la Integración Centroamericana (SICA) agreed a Code of Conduct on Arms Transfers. In 2006, West Africa's 15 presidents made a legally binding agreement to control small arms and light weapons transfers in their region, built on a voluntary moratorium of the Economic Community of West African States (ECOWAS) since 1998. This regional arms control treaty contains many provisions that could be used for a global Arms Trade Treaty.

There is no lack of national and regional initiatives to control the international transfer of arms.

There Are Few Global Controls

The only legally binding global agreements that explicitly apply to international transfers of arms are the UN [United Nations] Firearms Protocol (a supplement to the July 2000 UN Convention against Transnational Organised Crime), and occasional UN Security Council arms embargoes. Both have their limitations. The UN Firearms Protocol is restricted in scope to small arms and light weapons and does not apply to state-to-state transactions. It therefore does little to challenge current government policies or practices, and does not explicitly address the transfer of weapons by governments into regions in armed conflict or where they are likely to be used for human rights violations. It is however a legally binding agreement with potentially global application. UN arms embargoes are sometimes politically selective, and usually introduced when an arms-related humanitarian or human rights crisis is already under way. Moreover, implementation of these embargoes has been poor.

In July 2006, a UN conference on small arms and light weapons collapsed without agreement, despite the majority of governments, including those of the European Union [EU] and many African and Latin American governments, backing tougher controls on the international trade in small arms and light weapons. Due to the consensus decision-making process of this conference, a small number of countries, most notably the USA, who refused to countenance any further meetings, were able to block the outcome.

In short, there is no lack of national and regional initiatives to control the international transfer of arms. Most of these initiatives have been useful steps. But none of them has resulted in mechanisms to effectively control the supply of arms and dual-use equipment according to strict standards that would solve the problems outlined in this paper. In part, that is because they are merely national or regional initiatives to tackle what is increasingly a *global* trade.

Shortcomings of the Current Controls

Most of the above standards are merely political agreements; they are not legally binding treaties. Most are also regional in scope and only applicable to a limited number of states. They are open to interpretation by governments. Without legal force, they provide no sure way to hold governments to account for how vigorously or otherwise they enforce them.

In 1998, the EU's top four arms-exporting governments—France, Germany, Italy and the UK—refused 127 applications for export licences between them. In 2005, this rose to 217 refusals, an indication that implementing the Code of Conduct has caused these governments to refuse sensitive arms sales more often. However, EU countries continue to export arms to sensitive destinations where there is a risk that they will be used in contravention of EU Code criteria. In 2005, reports show that EU members licensed arms to China, Colombia, Ethiopia, Eritrea, Indonesia, Israel, Nepal and elsewhere. Without more detailed and transparent information about the nature of the arms supplied, how many, to whom they were sold and for what purpose, it is not possible to conclude that the EU Code of Conduct has managed to stop all arms exports that are likely to be used to fuel armed conflict, human rights abuses and poverty.

Moreover, as this paper has illustrated, the Code has done nothing to prevent European companies from exporting their production to countries such as Brazil, China or India, among others, from where weapons can be exported with relatively little control to prevent the use of these weapons to commit serious abuses. These countries' export controls do not include criteria or guidelines that reflect states' existing responsibilities under international human rights and humanitarian law.

In East and West Africa, where governments have now signed up to legally binding instruments, arms supplies keep coming because the treaties have yet to be translated into national law and enforcement practices. Until it was made legally binding, the 1998 West African small arms moratorium had limited effect, failing to prevent arms pouring into the brutal conflicts of Sierra Leone and Liberia up to 2002, and subsequently into Côote d'Ivoire. It remains to be seen whether the new legal instrument will be strong enough to make a difference in the region, but at least the regulations can now have a common and consistent legal footing, which should help law enforcers as well as parliamentarians, legal experts and civil society to hold the relevant states to account for their actions.

The Nairobi Protocol has yet to help improve the control of small arms in the Horn and East Africa. Some Best Practice Guidelines were agreed in 2005 that reflect state obligations under international law, but so far these have generally not been implemented and the arms trade in that region continues to fuel several deadly conflicts. In 2004, as war was ravaging both southern Sudan and Darfur, the Sudan government imported large quantities of arms. In the same year, Ethiopia and Eritrea faced each other on the edge of renewed conflict; and their joint arms race accounted for $364m of new weapons. Unsurprisingly, all three countries are among the 36 that spend more on their military than on health or education. In 2003, the populations of each of them had average life expectancy below 57 years.

A Global Treaty Is Necessary

All these codes, protocols and programmes have one element in common: none of them is a *global treaty*, apart from the UN Firearms Protocol, which has a very limited scope of application.

While the arms industry is more globalised than ever before, governments are languishing behind, in a world of national laws and regulations shaped by a weak set of regional and global standards, riddled with loopholes and poorly enforced. Compared to the global transformation of the industry, government controls seem painfully anachronistic when measured against the worldwide need for better human security.

However, governments are certainly aware of how the trade is changing. The US Department of Defense published its first major study on how to react to 'defence industry globalisation' in 1999. But after years—in some cases, decades—of the globalising processes described in this paper, states have still not developed binding global standards to regulate the international arms trade. In 2006, there are global treaties governing the trade in coffee, cocoa, timber, drugs, human beings and endangered species of flora and fauna. But there remains no such global treaty on conventional arms, parts and ammunition.

An International Arms Trade Treaty Is Feasible and Necessary

Arms Trade Treaty Steering Committee

The Arms Trade Treaty Steering Committee is an international group of nongovernmental organizations collaborating in the promotion of the Arms Trade Treaty at the national, regional, and international levels.

On 6 December 2006, the United Nations [UN] General Assembly voted in favour of taking first steps towards a legally-binding Arms Trade Treaty (ATT) to establish 'common international standards for the import, export and transfer of conventional arms'. The UN Resolution 61/89, adopted with the resounding support of 153 countries, is a landmark step towards a more effective regulation of the international arms trade.

There Is Support for an Arms Trade Treaty

Irresponsible and poorly regulated trade in arms fuels conflict, results in gross human rights abuses and serious violations of international humanitarian law (IHL), destabilises countries and regions and undermines sustainable development. For many years, NGOs [nongovernmental organizations] from around the world have raised awareness of the devastating impacts of poorly regulated arms transfers. In excess of a thousand people die each day as a result of armed violence with many more injured, displaced and traumatised. Whilst men are the main perpetrators and victims of armed violence,

Arms Trade Treaty Steering Committee, *Assessing the Feasibility, Scope and Parameters of an Arms Trade Treaty (ATT): An NGO Perspective*. Oxford: Oxfam, 2007, pp. 7–21. Copyright © 2007 Arms Trade Treaty Steering Committee. All rights reserved. Reproduced with the permission of Oxfam GB, Oxfam House, John Smith Drive, Cowley, Oxford OX4 2Jy UK, www.oxfam.org.uk. Oxfam GB does not necessarily endorse any text or activities that accompany the materials, nor has it approved the adapted text.

women and children suffer disproportionately from the destruction that attends the proliferation and misuse of conventional arms. Livelihoods are destroyed. Prospects for sustainable development are undermined. Insecurity is a fact of life for the millions who live in fear of armed violence. This has led many NGOs and governments to call for a global approach to controlling the arms trade.

Resolution 61/89 is welcomed by NGOs and other civil society groups who see this achievement as an important outcome of their international campaign for an ATT and the result of constructive dialogue and partnership between themselves and a significant number of governments.

An increasing number of governments are now vocal supporters of an ATT. Many more have expressed their willingness at the UN General Assembly to start the official negotiation process that will lead to an ATT. However, much still needs to be done before the support of the majority of UN member States translates into an effective international legally-binding treaty. The mutual benefits of constructive and sustainable partnerships between civil society, governments and various UN bodies will need to be pursued further. . . .

The Feasibility of an ATT

An ATT is feasible, as it would build on arms transfer principles that are now firmly established. Over the past decade, a significant amount has been achieved at the sub regional, regional and multilateral level to develop common standards for the regulation of international arms transfers. In particular, the Americas, Europe and Sub-Saharan Africa have adopted a number of comprehensive arms transfer control agreements. Whilst these agreements vary in their formulation and application, collectively they represent vital building blocks for a future ATT. . . .

The conclusion of a plethora of sub regional, regional and multilateral agreements to control the international transfer of conventional arms over the past decade reflects the growing realisation that the problem of such arms proliferation can only be effectively addressed through collaboration among States based upon the existing obligations of states. This applies both to those States involved in transferring arms internationally and those States affected by the impact of conventional arms proliferation and misuse. Further, a commitment to a global treaty to control the international transfer of conventional arms has been made by a significant number of Southern States by virtue of the November 2005 Commonwealth Heads of Government statement in which 38 Heads of Government noted the proposal for the development of common international standards for the trade in all conventional weapons and added their support to calls for work on such a treaty to commence at the UN.

Shared Standards in Existing Regional Controls

Overall, existing sub regional, regional and multilateral instruments for the control of international transfers of conventional arms address a similar-range of concerns, including the need to:

- Establish clear national procedures for regulating international transfers of arms;

- Prevent and combat illicit arms transfers;

- Respect UN arms embargoes;

- Prevent diversion to proscribed groups, such as those who commit terrorist or criminal acts;

- Prohibit transfers that violate obligations under international law;

- Prohibit transfers that are likely to be used for serious violations of human rights or international humanitarian law;

- Prohibit transfers that are likely to be used to commit crimes against humanity or acts of genocide;

- Prohibit transfers that adversely affect sustainable development;

- Prohibit transfers that are likely to adversely affect internal or regional security.

The overriding need to ensure respect for human rights and international humanitarian law in all arms transfers is particularly clear. Under the Principles and Purposes of the UN Charter all Member States have an obligation to encourage and promote universal respect for, and observance of, human rights and fundamental freedoms. Human rights include not only civil and political rights, but also economic, social and cultural rights—all of which are necessary for sustainable development.

Crucially, through their participation in regional and multilateral arms transfer control agreements, 118 States have already explicitly recognised that transfers of conventional arms including SALW [small arms and light weapons] should be refused where there is risk that they will contribute to serious breaches of human rights or gross violations of international humanitarian law. Moreover, in 2003, 191 States Parties to the Geneva Conventions undertook to make respect for international humanitarian law as one of the fundamental criteria on which arms transfer decisions are assessed and to incorporate such criteria into national laws or policies and into regional and global norms on arms transfers.

This level of existing agreement amongst a large number of States provides an important foundation for the development of an ATT which is reflective of States' core obligations under international law. Moreover, the recent conclusion of a legally-binding agreement on arms transfers by ECOWAS [Economic Community of West African States], the movement in the EU [European Union] towards adopting the EU

Code as a legally-binding instrument, together with the commitments contained in Section II, Paragraph 11 of the UN Small Arms Programme of Action are a clear indication of the increasing recognition amongst States that arms transfer controls should be rooted in International law.

Global Arms Control Is Necessary

Despite this progress, there remain gaps and weaknesses in the majority of regional and multilateral arms transfer control agreements, with attendant principles varying in formulation, failing to fully reflect the obligations that States have under international law and often being poorly enforced. Furthermore, there are a significant number of States that are not party to any regional or multilateral arms transfer control agreement. A global framework for arms transfer control is therefore a pressing priority.

While the need for agreement on global standards for control of the conventional arms trade is obvious, it is equally clear that such an agreement is feasible. States have already demonstrated through their collective work to address weapons of mass destruction that global agreements can be reached on the issue of weapons transfers. Moreover, the level of co-operation sub regionally, regionally and multilaterally in the field of conventional arms control is significant and growing. Finally, the vote on ATT Resolution 61/89 in the UN General Assembly makes clear that the overwhelming majority of States believe that the time for an ATT is now.

The Scope of an ATT

States have the right to acquire conventional arms for legitimate self-defence and law-enforcement needs in accordance with international law and standards. Resolution 61/89 acknowledges that this right is also accompanied by responsibilities. An ATT should not minimise or detract from this fundamental right of States but must recognise that there are other obligations that States have with respect to their transfers of arms.

An ATT should identify core substantive obligations that reflect existing international legal commitments on the part of States to:

- Prevent threats to the peace of the international community;

- Ensure respect for the laws of war; and

- Co-operate in the protection and fulfilment of human rights.

Accordingly, the use of conventional arms by States must comply inter alia [among other things] with international standards including those set by the United Nations Charter, the Geneva Conventions of 1949 (which also cover the actions of armed groups in a conflict) and the UN Basic Principles on the Use of Force and Firearms by Law Enforcement Officials of 1990.

Crucially, these responsibilities also extend to the transfer of conventional weapons. An ATT should reflect the scope of these obligations.

The prohibition of a weapon or a munition necessarily implies a prohibition on its transfer.

Restrictions and Prohibitions on Arms Transfers

The clearest example of restrictions on transfers of weapons is the imposition by the UN Security Council of arms embargoes on states and armed groups. Such decisions impose obligations on all United Nations Members.

There are also other international instruments that establish prohibitions on the transfer of particular types of weapons or munitions, such as anti-personnel landmines.

There are instruments that totally prohibit a particular kind of weapon, such as biological weapons.

The prohibition of a weapon or munition necessarily implies a prohibition on its transfer. A further group of international instruments impose an absolute prohibition on the use of particular types of weapons or munitions, for example, weapons with non-detectable fragments.

A blanket prohibition on the use of a weapon or munition must also imply a prohibition on the transfer of such a weapon or munition.

There are also limitations on the transfer of conventional arms which flow from the use or the likely use of such arms in particular circumstances. The responsibility of a State in such cases flows from its obligation, under international law, to not knowingly aid or assist another State in the commission of an unlawful act.

No country is immune from the risks of conventional arms proliferation.

Where a State has knowledge that weapons or munitions would be or would be likely to be used in breach of some fundamental principle of international law, the responsibility of the authorising State is to prohibit the proposed transfer. For example, where a State has knowledge that a transfer of weapons would be, or would be likely to be, used in the commission of genocide or of crimes against humanity, or in the commission of serious violations of international humanitarian or human rights law, the transferring State in question would itself commit an unlawful act, and be in violation of its international obligations, if it authorised the transfer in question.

What Should Be Covered by an ATT

The increasing globalisation of the international arms trade and its deleterious effects on sustainable development prospects has raised compelling arguments in favour of a global system of controls that comprehensively regulate all aspects of this trade. In order to be an effective global instrument, the ATT will need to comprise a comprehensive system to control the cross-border movement of all conventional arms and associated equipment. This should cover the import, export, transit and trans-shipment and brokerage of all conventional arms including:

- heavy weapons;

- small arms and light weapons;

- parts and components for the afore-mentioned;

- munitions including ammunition and explosives;

- technology used for manufacturing conventional arms;

- weapons used for internal security; and

- dual-use goods intended for military, security or policing [MSP] purposes. . . .

A Global Arms Trade Treaty Is Necessary for Security

Considering the danger posed to states and their populations by the persistent and flagrant misuse of weapons and munitions and at a time when the conventional arms trade has become increasingly global and differentiated in nature, no country is immune from the risks of conventional arms proliferation. States must therefore assist each other in preventing all types of conventional weapons, munitions, components, dual-use items and technology from falling into the wrong hands. A comprehensive global ATT based upon relevant principles of international law and standards should be the cornerstone of such a coordinated international effort.

To be effective, an ATT must be objective and allow for legitimate international transfers of conventional arms required for States' self defence and law enforcement needs in accordance with international law and standards. But to help reduce the proliferation and misuse of armaments, it must also incorporate operative provisions for the authorisation of international transfers that reflect States' existing obligations under relevant international law. An effective ATT must not dilute such obligations or contain ambiguous language that leads to different interpretations by states of those obligations.

Only such a global Arms Trade Treaty will overcome the current piecemeal approach of states attempting to use variable national and regional instruments to control international transfers of conventional arms and provide all states with the strong common international standards necessary to ensure a responsible arms trade. With the consequent reduction in the number of cases of weapons and munitions being diverted to those who undermine human, national and international security, such an ATT will greatly benefit not only those communities, states and regions where arms proliferation and misuse are widespread, but would also improve the prospects for increased security worldwide.

The United States Should Support an Arms Trade Treaty

William D. Hartung

William D. Hartung is director of the arms and security initiative at the New America Foundation, and is the author of And Weapons for All, *a book about America's multibillion-dollar arms trade.*

While the U.S. hangs its foreign policy on preventing the spread of "weapons of mass destruction" (a worthy goal, however grossly the Bush administration goes about achieving it), it continues to ignore a more immediate threat—the proliferation of small arms and light weapons—that deserves serious attention as well. These low-tech arms have been described as "slow motion weapons of mass destruction," because they are responsible for hundreds of thousands of deaths over the past dozen years, from the genocide in Rwanda to the ongoing civil war in the Democratic Republic of the Congo. Yet yesterday [October 26, 2006], the United States, the world's largest arms supplier, voted against an historic United Nations [U.N.] proposal to curb traffic in arms.

An Arms Trade Treaty Proposal

The United Nations vote was the culmination of the work of a network of prominent individuals and diverse non-governmental organizations. They set out to address the problem of small arms and light weapons—as well as larger systems like tanks, fighter planes and attack helicopters—by putting forward a proposal for an Arms Trade Treaty. The thrust of the proposed treaty is to curb arms transfers to major human rights abusers and areas of conflict. It would also

William D. Hartung, "We Arm the World," *TomPaine.com*, October 27, 2006. (A Project of The Institute for America's Future). Reproduced by permission.

urge weapons suppliers to limit weapons sales that are likely to undermine development in poor nations.

Other elements of an arms treaty could include the creation of common international criteria for assessing particular exports, and movement toward global enforcement mechanisms such as licensing of the arms brokers and shippers who are all too often at the center of illegal deals that have fueled conflicts in Liberia, Sierra Leone, Angola and Rwanda.

As a first step—by a vote of 139 to 1 with 24 abstentions—the U.N. General Assembly agreed yesterday [October 26, 2006] to create a two-part process aimed at pursuing such a treaty. The United States was the only vote in opposition to the resolution.

A treaty will be an historic step forward in the global arms control regime.

Now, as a result of the successful vote, the first step will be a survey of U.N. member states by the secretary general's office. The survey will seek the views of U.N. members on the feasibility and practicality of a legally binding treaty that would set international standards on arms transfers. In 2008, these same questions will be addressed by a group of experts that will delve more deeply into the subject.

U.S. Security Is Harmed by Lack of a Treaty

However long it takes, a treaty will be an historic step forward in the global arms control regime. Up until now, the arms trade has been the "orphan of arms control"—bound by no international treaties of the sort that govern the possession or spread of nuclear, chemical and biological weaponry.

How can it be that the Bush administration was the only government in the world that voted against even *thinking* about an Arms Trade Treaty? U.S. security has suffered more harm than good from the widespread availability of small arms and light weapons, which often end up being used against U.S. troops. A recent study by researchers at Johns Hopkins University has found that over half of U.S. casualties in Iraq have been inflicted by AK-47s.

In fact, American-made weapons also frequently end up pointing at American soldiers. For example, the early foundations of al-Qaida were built in part on relationships and weaponry that came from the billions of dollars in U.S. support for the Afghan mujahadin during the war to expel Soviet forces from that country. U.S. military personnel in Somalia and Panama faced U.S.-supplied weaponry that had been given to those nations when they were U.S. allies. In Panama, the issue at hand was a change in Panamanian and U.S. government policies. In Somalia, warlords got hold of U.S.-origin weapons in the wake of the overthrow of the Siad Barre dictatorship. These patterns are likely to continue if nothing is done to stem the wholesale trade in weapons.

The United States has a special responsibility to take the lead in regulating the trade.

The specific impacts of runaway arms trafficking on U.S. forces are amplified by broader concerns. Relatively inexpensive and readily available small arms and light weapons can be used to destabilize countries, creating political chaos and economic devastation. In turn this can contribute to making these countries havens for terrorism while undermining their ability to achieve economic self-sufficiency and accountable governments.

The Reasons for U.S. Opposition

So, the question remains, why is the United States opposed to taking measures to stop this deadly trade? The first answer is strategic. The executive branch wants to preserve its "freedom of action" to arm U.S.-allied groups like the Nicaraguan contras, the Afghan mujahadin, Jonas Savimbi's UNITA movement in Angola, the Iraqi National Congress and groups opposed to the current regime in Iran. Even if one accepts the right of the United States to attempt to overthrow governments that oppose its short-term political or economic imperatives—which this author does not—the short-term "benefits" of these arms-supply relationships are inevitably outweighed by the long-term costs to U.S. and global interests. Unfortunately, short-sighted policymakers in Washington—of both parties—have failed to understand or accept this fundamental principle.

As the world's number one arms exporting nation, the United States has a special responsibility to take the lead in regulating the trade. A 2005 report by the World Policy Institute found that of the largest U.S. arms recipients in the developing world, over 70 percent were undemocratic regimes, major human rights abusers or both.

The United States is not alone in the business of unsavory arms exports. A recent report by the research group Safeworld found that in the past year, the United Kingdom provided weapons to 19 of 20 nations that had been singled out by its own government as "major countries of concern" for human rights abuses. And the Control Arms Campaign has found Russian, Greek, Chinese and U.S.-origin bullets in the Democratic Republic of the Congo, which is engaged in one of the deadliest civil wars in living memory.

A second factor in U.S. opposition to any substantial measures to curb the weapons trade is the role of the domestic gun lobby. Both the National Rifle Association and its allied organization, the World Forum on the Future of Sport Shooting Activities, have gone on record against an Arms Trade Treaty. National Rifle Association propaganda has made the false claim that a treaty would lead to the confiscation of guns owned by U.S. citizens.

The Rest of the World Is Moving Ahead

The good news is that, despite U.S. opposition, the U.N. General Assembly has voted to support steps towards the creation of a treaty regulating the arms trade. This is due in large part to the strenuous efforts of organizations like Amnesty International, Oxfam and the International Action Network on Small Arms, which includes over 500 member organizations in more than 100 countries.

There is a long way to go before there will be an international treaty curbing the arms trade, but this week's action at the United Nations is an important step forward, and an indication that progress can be made even in the face of opposition by the Bush administration and the gun lobby. A change in U.S. policy is urgently needed, but in the meantime the rest of the world is moving ahead without us.

There Are Alternatives to International Arms Control Treaties

Baker Spring

Baker Spring is the F.M. Kirby Research Fellow in National Security Policy in the Kathryn and Shelby Cullom Davis Institute for International Studies at the Heritage Foundation, a research institute dedicated to promoting conservative public policies.

B y spearheading the Proliferation Security Initiative (PSI), the Bush Administration has taken a major step toward balancing international and national authority in controlling weapons proliferation. The PSI seeks to coordinate the actions of individual states in interdicting shipments of weapons, weapons components, and weapons production equipment.

International Treaties Are Not the Only Option

This approach allows each participating state to make a contribution toward interdicting relevant shipments in a way that is consistent with its national laws and policies. By sidestepping the "least-common-denominator" approach for establishing international non-proliferation policy that is inherent in the consensus-based decision-making process of an international treaty regime, the PSI has already demonstrated that it will make a powerful contribution toward stemming proliferation.

As a means of hindering proliferation, multilateral arms control has become too dependent on a treaty regime managed by cumbersome international bureaucracies. This depen-

Baker Spring, "Harnessing the Power of Nations for Arms Control: The Proliferation Security Initiative and Coalitions of the Willing," *Backgrounder No. 1737 (Heritage Foundation)*, March 18, 2004, pp. 1–2, 4–5, 9. Copyright © 2004 The Heritage Foundation. Reproduced by permission.

dency weakens the critical effort to control the proliferation of biological, chemical, and nuclear weapons and their delivery systems by depriving it of needed flexibility and access to a wider variety of tools. Augmenting the treaty regime and its institutions—e.g., the Biological Weapons Convention (BWC), the Chemical Weapons Convention (CWC), the Comprehensive Test Ban Treaty (CTBT), the Nuclear Non-Proliferation Treaty (NPT), the Organization for the Prohibition of Chemical Weapons (OPCW), and the International Atomic Energy Agency (IAEA)—necessarily depends on encouraging individual states to exercise their sovereign authority to control proliferation.

Non-proliferation should not remain an effort in which centralized international authorities seek to override state sovereignty. Rather, the international treaty regime should share with national authorities the responsibility for addressing proliferation threats. . . .

The international treaty-based regime for combating proliferation could use some healthy competition.

Guidelines for the Future of Arms Control

Given the early indications of success under the PSI, the U.S. and other participating states should use it as a basis for continuing to expand the tools for combating proliferation. In reality, the PSI represents a new approach to arms control: an approach designed not to *replace* the existing treaty-based regime, but to *augment* it by expanding the arms control effort. Given the current context, the ongoing effort to build and strengthen the PSI should be directed by the following guidelines:

Guideline #1: Foster healthy competition with the institutions of the treaty-based non-proliferation regime.

The treaty-based international non-proliferation regime should not have monopolistic powers. With few exceptions, this regime has dominated the world of arms control in the area of non-proliferation. As a result, it exhibits the classic weaknesses associated with any monopoly. It is large, slow, complacent, and lacking in creativity. It is easily distracted and drawn into matters tangential to its primary purpose. The bureaucracies that manage the regime seem more interested in self-protection and perpetuation than in meeting new demands.

The following are just some of the shortcomings that have surfaced with the treaty-based regime and its affiliated bureaucracies over the years:

- Debate over the NPT has become more focused on the tangential issue of "general and complete disarmament" than on the object and purpose of the treaty, which is stemming the spread of nuclear weapons.

- The BWC is inherently unverifiable. Nevertheless, considerable effort was put into the unachievable goal of crafting a verification protocol to the treaty. Predictably, this effort failed in July 2001.

- The CWC is unenforceable. The result is that significant chemical arsenals will remain intact for the foreseeable future, despite the treaty's assertion that it will "exclude completely the possibility of the use of chemical weapons." The CWC represents a wet blanket for creative efforts to address the enduring chemical weapons threat.

- The CTBT will not be brought into force, but this fact has had little impact on those pursuing a futile effort to find a magic formula for bringing it into force. As a result, the CTBT has become yet another distraction in the effort to stem nuclear proliferation.

- The OPCW Director General was dismissed for mismanagement in 2002.

- The IAEA underestimated the scope of the Iraqi nuclear weapons program in the late 1980s and early 1990s.

Clearly, the international treaty-based regime for combating proliferation could use some healthy competition. Thus, the PSI should not be pursued as a replacement for the treaty-based regime but as a supplement. Under Secretary of State John Bolton has confirmed the U.S. government's intention to participate in the PSI on this basis.

In essence, the PSI—and any additional non-proliferation initiatives or activities of a similar nature—should serve as a force to counter the monopolistic behavior present in the treaty-based regime. In effect, they should represent new entrepreneurial players in the non-proliferation arms control market. Institutions such as the NPT, the CWC, the IAEA, and the OPCW should be forced to compete.

Guideline #2: Resist the temptation to build cumbersome international bureaucracies.

Under Secretary of State John Bolton has noted on several occasions that the PSI is "an activity rather than an organization." This is appropriate. As noted earlier, the PSI has resulted in a series of substantive exercises and actual interdiction operations, despite commencing less than a year ago. This has been possible because the member states are focused on their interdiction activities and not on building a bureaucracy.

The OPCW, by comparison, is seven years old and, by its own account, has been focused on building an international bureaucracy. The OPCW Web site boasts that the organization has 158 member countries (as of the end of 2003) and a staff of 500 people from 66 countries, communicates in six different languages, spends about 60 million euros annually, and forces "big, rich countries" to finance the majority of its operations while "some smaller and/or poorer countries pay as little as one thousandth of one percent of the budget." Clearly, the OPCW leadership is not focused on fashioning a "lean and mean" organization that is results-oriented.

As the PSI matures, however, pressure to "institutionalize" will likely grow. This pressure should be resisted. Building an international bureaucracy will only distract PSI participating states from performing the essential function of interdicting weapons-related shipments. The same bias against institution-alization should be applied to any future PSI-related compan-ion initiatives. . . .

International Arms Control Efforts Are Not Enough

The nation-state remains the primary component of the inter-national system. The extent to which the international non-proliferation effort fails to account for this fact is the extent to which the effort is weakened. The PSI works within the struc-ture of the nation-state system. It reinforces national sover-eignty rather than weakening sovereignty by vesting enforce-ment authority in some supranational body like the United Nations. As a result, it strengthens the forces for non-proliferation worldwide by harnessing the strengths of the nation-state system.

If arms control is left completely in the hands of ineffec-tive and unaccountable international bureaucracies, this essential tool of non-proliferation will atrophy.

Further, today's world is more complex and less predict-able than during the Cold War. As a result, rigidly structured international coalitions cannot effectively respond to the rapid pace of threatening developments. The appropriate response is to create less formal and more loosely structured international coalitions that are more responsive and adaptive. This is the case with arms control as well as with military operations. The PSI shows how the coalitions-of-the-willing concept can be applied to arms control and non-proliferation.

The attacks of September 11, 2001, serve as a warning to civilized nations of the intolerable risks associated with the unchecked proliferation of biological, chemical, and nuclear weapons and the missiles to deliver them. While arms control is only one of several tools for combating proliferation, it is an essential one. If arms control is left completely in the hands of ineffective and unaccountable international bureaucracies, this essential tool of non-proliferation will atrophy. The PSI serves to ensure that such an unfortunate outcome is not the result.

An Arms Trade Treaty Could Encourage Human Rights Violations

David B. Kopel, Paul Gallant, and Joanne D. Eisen

David B. Kopel is research director for the Independence Institute. Paul Gallant and Joanne D. Eisen are senior fellows at the Independence Institute.

While the United Nations [UN] works diligently to curb the Second Amendment rights of Americans, it is turning a blind eye to abused Karamojong tribesmen fighting a brutal government to keep their only means of self-defense.

The Arms Trade Treaty and Gun Control

International gun prohibition groups are working hard and successfully to push an Arms Trade Treaty (ATT) through the United Nations. They claim that the reason the treaty is needed is that arms are often used to violate human rights.

True enough. One need only look at Burma, where the military dictatorship has been torturing and killing Buddhist monks and other pro-rights activists. Burma, by the way, has a strict gun control law dating back to 1951: The president can ban any gun by fiat [arbitrary decree], and any person possessing a banned gun is presumed guilty of high treason and must prove his innocence.

One thing that the media doesn't tell you about the Arms Trade Treaty is that an important goal of its proponents is an international legal ban on the sale of arms, including components for making guns, to Israel. Control Arms is a gun control lobby jointly created by the International Action Network

David B. Kopel, Paul Gallant, and Joanne D. Eisen, "Uganda: We're From the Government and We're Here to Help You," *America's 1st Freedom*, vol. 9, January 2008, pp. 36–39, 60. Copyright © 2008 David B. Kopel, Paul Gallant, and Joanne D. Eisen. Reproduced by permission.

on Small Arms (IANSA), Amnesty International and Oxfam. In November 2006, Control Arms issued "Arms Without Borders," a document setting forth the case for the Arms Trade Treaty, and describing Israel as one the countries that the ATT would target.

Nor does the media point out that another target of the ATT is the United States, since our gun and self-defense laws are—according to the UN Human Rights Commission—violations of international human rights. American crime victims and police officers can use firearms to defend against non-lethal attacks, such as attacks by rapists, armed robbers or home arsonists. Yet according to the UN, allowing a woman to save herself from rape by shooting the rapist is a human rights violation.

But the most glaring omission in the discussion of the Arms Trade Treaty as a human rights tool is the complete silence about how gun control has so often been used to violate human rights. Consider, for example, what's going on right now in Uganda.

Their only protection from government predators with guns was keeping defensive guns themselves.

The Questionable Link Between Gun Ownership and Violence

The borderlands of northeastern Uganda, northwestern Kenya, southeastern Sudan and southwestern Ethiopia are occupied by the tribes of the pastoral Karamojong people. Cattle herds are the center of their culture, and provide the major source of dietary protein from milk, blood and meat. Wealth and local political power are based on the size of one's cattle herd. For countless generations, cattle rustling has been a traditional Karamojong pursuit.

The UN and its disarmament cronies have recently claimed that the availability of modern arms has made cattle raiding deadlier and that civilian gun ownership is the root cause of the area's problems.

Not so, replies Ben Knighton, who is dean of the research program at the Oxford Centre for Mission Studies, and author of the book *The Vitality of Karamojong Religion: Dying Tradition or Living Faith?* Knighton argues that the Ugandan army's gun confiscation program is itself the major cause of violence.

Even Kilfemarian Gebre-Wold, former director of a voluntary gun surrender program sponsored by Germany's Bonn International Center for Conversion, forthrightly acknowledges that "though many pastoralist households have small arms, the rate of crime and violent incidents is not high in their community . . . the density of weapons does not mean automatically the rise of gun-related violence."

The History of Gun Control in Uganda

Unfortunately, these humanitarians do not make policy. Milton Obote, Uganda's first prime minister, imposed a nationwide ban on the civilian possession of firearms in 1969. General Idi Amin later overthrew Obote, and, thanks to Obote's previous gun control work, was able to perpetrate genocide, killing hundreds of thousands of Ugandans, especially in Karamoja. The Karamojong tried to fight back using steel tubing from furniture to fabricate crude firearms.

The Tanzanian army invaded Uganda and overthrew Amin in 1979. While Amin's army was collapsing in the face of the Tanzanian invasion and the subsequent chaos, the Karamojong found easy access to deserted government armories filled with modern weapons.

Julius Nyerere, the dictator of Tanzania, restored Obote as dictator of Uganda. Obote quickly resumed his attempts to disarm the Karamojong. His efforts were often forcefully repelled, because the Karamojong had learned that cows and guns are equally indispensable—a gun needs to be readily accessible in order to protect one's herd. Obote retaliated by using his army and secret police to brutalize the tribes.

In 1984, the Ugandan and Kenyan armies collaborated in Operation Nyundo ("Hammer") to eliminate armed herders seeking cross-border safety. Lepokoy Kolimuk, a village elder in Kanyarkwat village, Kenya, said the soldiers were "wild beyond humanity." The number of human deaths remains unknown. Twenty thousand cattle were rounded up and starved to death. Nevertheless, Operation Nyundo failed to disarm the Karamojong.

In 1986, strongman Yoweri Museveni toppled Obote and continued the violent firearms confiscation. The army, with the wildly inaccurate title of Uganda People's Defence Forces (UPDF) abused civilians by looting supplies and raping women. The UPDF's actions confirmed to the Karamojong that their only protection from government predators with guns was keeping defensive guns themselves. The resistance was so great that Museveni temporarily abandoned his disarmament efforts in 1989.

Yet prompted by the UN, Museveni got back into the gun control business in 2001, with a voluntary gun surrender program. The program expired on Feb. 15, 2002, and only 7,676 guns (out of a conservatively estimated 40,000 in Karamojong hands) were collected.

Attempted Disarmament Created More Violence

In order to confiscate the rest of the firearms, the army recommenced what the international gun-ban lobbies euphemistically call "forcible disarmament." Rape, torture and the destruction of homes after systematic army looting became commonplace.

Father Declan O'Toole, a member of the Mill Hill Missionaries, asked the army to be "less aggressive." Just a few days later, on March 21, 2002, he was murdered by UPDF soldiers. The murderers were apprehended and executed before they could reveal who had given them the order to kill Father O'Toole. Uganda President Museveni blamed the Karamojong, claiming, "The best way to stop such incidents in [the] future is for the Karamojong to hand in their guns to eliminate any justification for the UPDF operations in the villages."

The disarmament only created a new group of victims, who were preyed upon by those who still had firearms.

In the northern district of Kotido, the Ugandan army engaged armed civilians and captured about 30 rifles on May 16. Thirteen civilians and two soldiers died—one person dead for every two guns confiscated. Thousands of residents were displaced because their homes were torched by UPDF troops.

By mid-July of 2002, the total number of guns recovered by the government, from both the voluntary and forced gun surrender programs, had reached nearly 10,000, leaving tens of thousands of guns still in Karamojong hands.

Museveni had promised to increase security for people who gave up their guns, but that promise proved empty. The disarmament only created a new group of victms, who were preyed upon by those who still had firearms. There were many instances of violence against the disarmed, by both civilians and soldiers. After homes were bombed and crops were destroyed, thousands of tribespeople fled across the border to Kenya. About 80,000 more people were internally displaced.

Despite all the suffering inflicted on the Karamojong, the disarmament program failed. In 2002, the pro-government Ugandan newspaper New Vision acknowledged that the Karamojong were now "purchasing more guns to replenish those either voluntarily handed [over] or forcefully recovered by the government."

Another Kenya-Uganda military assault on Karamoja's gun-owning villages was launched in 2005, but in 2006, Col. Phenehas Katirima, chief of personnel and administration in the UPDF, admitted, "Brand new guns from western Europe, across the Mediterranean and the Middle East have been seen in Karamoja."

The UN's Reaction to Violence in Uganda

Because of the human rights atrocities, the United Nations Development Programme temporarily suspended its funding of the Ugandan development and voluntary disarmament programs. (The UN had never funded the military program, except to the extent that money is fungible, and foreign aid is often diverted by corrupt governments.)

Still, the Ugandan army's campaign persisted. On Oct. 29, 2006, the UPDF attempted to disarm the village of Lopuyo, but was repulsed after an 8-hour battle with armed Karamojong. Army spokesman Major Felix Kulaije stated that, in the course of retrieving firearms, "we went there peacefully in a cordon and search operation." However, the villagers told a more harrowing story. The army surrounded the village and began to question and torture young men. Still, few guns were recovered, and the tribesmen began to attack the UPDF.

The UPDF then launched retaliatory raids on the Karamojong using a helicopter gunship, but found that they no longer had complete control of the airspace. Some of the new weapons the Karamojong had acquired were capable of hitting aircraft.

On Nov. 10, 2006, the UN news agency Integrated Regional Information Networks (IRIN) reported that the village of Kadokini was targeted. "UPDF tanks then drove through the village crushing and damaging properties, including huts and granaries." The result was three deaths, seven acts of torture and five guns confiscated by the army. Many similar attacks have also been reported by the UN and local newspapers.

Yet the UN—which seems to be more in favor of gun control schemes than opposed to gross human rights violations—has not demanded that Museveni reign in his troops. Instead, according to the UN's acting humanitarian coordinator in Uganda, Theophane Nikyema: "The United Nations . . . appeals to Karamojong communities to refrain from violent responses to law and order efforts." With alliances forming among the tribes in order to defeat their common enemy—their government—it does not appear that they are willing to disarm, but are instead preparing for further violent resistance.

The Ugandan government continues its own efforts to increase the number of cold, dead hands among the Karamojong.

The UN's news service did admit on May 30, 2007, that, "Intermittent efforts to disarm, sometimes forcibly, up to 20 million pastoralists in the Horn of Africa, who are believed to possess 5 million firearms, have failed . . . and forcible disarmament has not worked."

It's doubtful that a single Karamojong man or woman has ever heard of former NRA President Charlton Heston. Yet the Karamojong people plainly share his sentiment: "From my cold, dead hands."

Gun Control Can Lead to Human Rights Violations

In the meantime, the Ugandan government continues its own efforts to increase the number of cold, dead hands among the Karamojong. Ugandan Gen. Aronda Nyakairima states that the UPDF is ready to use "any available means" to get civilian guns. According to a report of the United Nations High Commissioner for Human Rights, "The UPDF continues to engage in acts which ultimately result in human rights violations, including killings, injuries, torture, damages and destruction of property and livelihoods." The UPDF attacks take place not only in Uganda, but also in Karamojong regions of Kenya.

The UN personnel who have reported on the human rights abuses in Uganda's gun control campaign deserve respect. It is unfortunate that Control Arms, Amnesty International, Oxfam and IANSA have said nothing about the Ugandan army's gun control depredations against the Karamojong. It's not as if they're unaware of the problem; we hand-delivered our previous report on the problem to them in July 2007 at the UN gun control conference. It was during the same conference that the UN cut off funding for Uganda—an act that was not exactly kept secret from the people at the conference.

If the true purpose of the Arms Trade Treaty is really to protect human rights—rather than to set the stage for arms embargos on the U.S. and Israel—the treaty will need to address the problem of arms possessed by armies like the UPDF and the human rights atrocities they perpetrate in the name of gun control.

An International Agreement on Small Arms Would Violate the U.S. Constitution's Second Amendment

Joseph Klein

Joseph Klein is the author of Global Deception: The UN's Stealth Assault on America's Freedom.

As our Independence Day celebration approaches, the United Nations [UN] is holding a global conference in New York, starting on June 26th [2006] and lasting through July 7th, whose real agenda is to begin a backdoor process of interference with our constitutionally protected right to individually bear arms. The UN denies this, of course. It says that the only purpose of the conference is to *review progress made in the implementation* of the Programme of Action to Prevent, Combat and Eradicate the *Illicit* Trade in Small Arms and Light Weapons in All Its Aspects that was adopted in 2001. Faced with over 100,000 letters of protest about the review conference from American citizens concerned about holding on to their freedoms, the conference chairman—Prasad Kariyawasam, Sri Lanka's U.N. ambassador—said that this year's review conference will deal only with illegal arms and *"does not in any way address legal possession."* The review conference's website says that *"it is not the wish of nations attending the Conference to discuss outlawing the legal manufacture or trade of these weapons, nor their legal ownership."*

The UN's Position on Small Arms

The review conference's backers blame the National Rifle Association, whose executive vice president, Wayne LaPierre, came out recently with a book entitled *The Global War on Your Guns*, for inflaming passions by distorting what the review conference is intended to accomplish. Unfortunately for American citizens, however, the NRA is right. The United Nations and its well-heeled backers are playing word games to cover their true intentions, as they always do. This is the typical 'stealth' strategy that I discuss at length in my book, *Global Deception*. Here we find Chairman Kariyawasam, and the gun prohibitionist crowd who are pulling the strings for the review conference from behind the scenes, caught in a web of deception of their own making.

In his so-called "*non-paper for informal consultation purposes*" dated May 18, 2006 (yes folks, only the United Nations can call a document of 10 pages of recommendations a 'non-paper'), Chairman Kariyawasam recommended as one concrete measure that "*States that have not already done so*" should "*adopt adequate laws, regulations and administrative procedures to regulate the possession of small arms and light weapons.*" This 'non-paper' is intended to serve as the basis for an eventual 'Outcome Document' approved by the review committee. The Outcome Document, in turn, will no doubt be characterized as the UN's official implementing interpretation of the Programme of Action. Note that the reference to the regulation of the possession of small arms had been proposed and rejected when the Programme of Action itself was adopted in 2001, but its backers are seeking to restore the idea through the back door of the review conference's Outcome Document.

The United States will block any legally binding treaty that contains a reference to regulation of possession of small arms.

IANSA Is Against the Right to Bear Arms

Predictably, the anti-gun possession fanatic Rebecca Peters, who is Director of the International Action Network on Small

Arms (IANSA)—a network of more than 700 non-governmental organizations working in 100 countries against the individual's right to bear arms—has seized on this opening. IANSA is the official coordinator of non-governmental organizations' involvement in the UN small arms process. Its sources of funding include the Ford Foundation, Rockefeller Foundation, and George Soros' Open Society Institute. IANSA is already guaranteed to have a seat at the table, but it is pressing for a fuller partnership with the member state delegations in the review conference's deliberations.

In her response to Chairman Kariyawasam's 'non-paper', Peters wrote that IANSA welcomed *"the reference to regulating the possession of small arms and light weapons"* but urged that it be expanded. She also raised the gun prohibition specter explicitly, recommending the outright prohibition of semi-automatic and automatic rifles and declaring that *"(M)any States already prohibit the civilian possession of light weapons, and this should be recognised in the paragraph devoted to light weapons control."*

We should . . . celebrate our Declaration of Independence by telling the gun prohibitionists . . . to either stay out of our business or stay out of our country.

Peters knows that the United States will block any legally binding treaty that contains a reference to regulation of possession of small arms. However, she is doing all that she can to get a UN-sponsored international norm against individual gun possession on the record somehow—what IANSA in the past has referred to as *"norms of non-possession."* She claims that many member states are calling for the review conference's Outcome Document to recognize the critical importance of national gun laws and to suggest guidelines or standards for such laws. Indeed, IANSA has the backing of an intergovernmental organization known as *The Parliamentary Fo-*

rum on Small Arms and Light Weapons which, according to its website, was created to serve as an international platform for parliamentarians interested in small arms related work, to contribute to the advancement of the small arms agenda, and *"to provide space for parliamentarians and civil society to meet and join forces"*. The Parliamentary Forum is in complete synch with Rebecca Peters' IANSA agenda. It proposed a 'Model Parliamentary Resolution on Small Arms and Light Weapons' that resolved to *"strongly recommend that governments prohibit the civilian possession and use of all light weapons and automatic and semi-automatic rifles and machine guns."*

Gun Ownership Is a Second Amendment Right

Peters' strategy, with the help of the chairman of the UN review conference and the Parliamentary Forum, is to enshrine international norms against civilian gun possession in an interpretive document that gun prohibitionists can label 'customary international law.' Such a document would legitimize Peters' dogma that *"gun ownership is not a right but a privilege."* IANSA can then use the international norms in our own courts to attack the notion that an individual right to bear arms is enshrined in the Second Amendment. They are counting on sympathetic federal judges, right up to the Supreme Court, to interpret the scope of the Second Amendment's protections by deferring to 'international norms' against individual gun possession. In short, the stealth strategy here is for IANSA to drive the UN review conference's agenda, obtain the wording they seek on curtailing private gun possession in the review conference's official Outcome Document that they can point to as an 'international norm', and then argue that this 'international norm' should be incorporated into our courts' interpretation of the Second Amendment—*converting a constitutionally protected individual right into a government-bestowed privilege.*

Ironically, IANSA is headquartered in London. One of its UK-based member organizations called International Alert showed no compunction at all in boldly declaring that *"the U.S. Constitution does not guarantee individuals the right to possess or carry guns."* Apparently some British folks have forgotten from whom we won our freedom—and why we sought it in the first place. We should as a nation celebrate our Declaration of Independence by telling the gun prohibitionists who are assembling in New York from all over the world during our Independence Day holiday to either stay out of our business or stay out of our country.

An End to the Arms Trade, Not More Regulation, Is Needed

Frida Berrigan

Frida Berrigan is a senior research associate at the World Policy Institute's Arms Trade Resource Center.

They don't call us the sole superpower for nothing. Paul Wolfowitz might be looking for a new job right now, but the term he used to describe the pervasiveness of U.S. power back when he was a mere deputy secretary of Defense—hyperpower—still fits the bill. Consider some of the areas in which the United States is still No. 1:

- First in weapons sales: Since 2001, U.S. global military sales have totaled $10 billion to $13 billion. That's a lot of weapons, but in fiscal 2006, the Pentagon broke its own recent record, inking arms sales agreements worth $21 billion.

- First in sales of surface-to-air missiles: From 2001 to 2005, the U.S. delivered 2,099 surface-to-air missiles like the Sparrow and AMRAAM [Advanced Medium-Range Air-to-Air Missle] to nations in the developing world, 20% more than Russia, the next largest supplier.

- First in sales of military ships: During that same period, the U.S. sent 10 "major surface combatants," such as aircraft carriers and destroyers, to developing nations. Collectively, the four major European weapons producers shipped 13.

- First in military training: A thoughtful empire knows that it's not enough to send weapons; you have to teach

Frida Berrigan, "America—The World's Arms Pusher," *Los Angeles Times*, May 21, 2007. Copyright © 2007 *Los Angeles Times*. Reproduced by permission of the author.

people how to use them. The Pentagon plans on training the militaries of 138 nations in 2008 at a cost of nearly $90 million. No other nation comes close.

There Is a Huge Market for U.S. Weapons

Rest assured, governments around the world, often at each others' throats, will want U.S. weapons long after their people have turned up their noses at a range of once dominant American consumer goods. The "trade" publication *Defense News*, for instance, recently reported that Turkey and the U.S. signed a $1.78-billion deal for Lockheed Martin F-16 fighter planes. As it happens, these planes are already ubiquitous—Israel flies them; so does the United Arab Emirates, Poland, South Korea, Venezuela, Oman and Portugal, among others. Buying our weaponry is one of the few ways you can actually join the American imperial project!

In order to remain on top in the competitive jet field, Lockheed Martin, for example, does far more than just sell airplanes. TAI—Turkey's aerospace corporation—will receive a boost with this sale because Lockheed Martin is handing over responsibility for portions of production, assembly and testing to Turkish workers.

Our most successful (and most deadly) export remains our most invisible one.

The Turkish air force already has 215 F-16 fighter planes and plans to buy 100 of Lockheed Martin's new F-35 Joint Strike Fighter as well, in a deal estimated at $10.7 billion over the next 15 years. That's $10.7 billion on fighter planes for a country that ranks 94th on the United Nations' human development index, below Lebanon, Colombia and Grenada and far below all the European nations that Ankara is courting as it seeks to join the European Union. Now that's a real American sales job for you!

Here's the strange thing, though: This genuine, gold-medal manufacturing-and-sales job on weapons simply never gets the attention it deserves. As a result, most Americans have no idea how proud they should be of our weapons manufacturers and the Pentagon—essentially our global sales force. They make sure our weapons travel the planet and regularly demonstrate their value in small wars from Latin America to Central Asia.

The Market for Weapons is Manufactured

There's tons of data on the weapons trade, but who knows about any of it? I help produce one of a dozen or so sober annual (or semiannual) reports quantifying the business of warmaking, so I know that these reports get desultory, obligatory media attention. Only once in a blue moon do they get the sort of full-court-press treatment that befits our No. 1 product line.

We don't need stronger arms control laws, we need a global sobriety coach and some kind of 12-step program for the dealer-nation as well.

Even when there is coverage, the inside-the-fold, fact-heavy, wonky news stories on the arms trade, however useful, can't possibly convey the feel of a business that has always preferred the shadows to the sun. The connection between the factory that makes a weapons system and the community where that weapon "does its duty" is invariably missing in action, as are the relationships among the companies making the weapons and the generals (on-duty and retired) and politicians making the deals, or raking in their own cuts of the profits for themselves and/or their constituencies. In other words, our most successful (and most deadly) export remains our most invisible one.

Maybe the only way to break through this paralysis of analysis would be to stop talking about weapons sales as a trade and the export of precision-guided missiles as if they were so many widgets. Maybe we need to start thinking about them in another language entirely—the language of drugs.

After all, what does a drug dealer do? He creates a need and then fills it. He encourages an appetite or (even more lucratively) an addiction and then feeds it.

Arms dealers do the same thing. They suggest to foreign officials that their military just might need a slight upgrade. After all, they'll point out, haven't you noticed that your neighbor just upgraded in jets, submarines and tanks? And didn't you guys fight a war a few years back? Doesn't that make you feel insecure? And why feel insecure for another moment when, for just a few billion bucks, we'll get you suited up with the latest model military, even better than what we sold them—or you the last time around.

Why do officials in Turkey, which already has 215 fighter planes, need 100 extras in an even higher-tech version? They don't, but Lockheed Martin, working with the Pentagon, made them think they did.

We don't need stronger arms control laws, we need a global sobriety coach and some kind of 12-step program for the dealer-nation as well.

CHAPTER 4

What Are Some of the Concerns About the Arms Trade?

Chapter Preface

The former Belgian colony of the Belgian Congo became the Democratic Republic of the Congo in 1960. And, since the toppling of the regime of President Joseph Mobutu in 1997, the country has been involved in civil war and conflicts with neighboring countries. Despite peace accords in 2002, conflict has continued in the Democratic Republic of the Congo, and the United Nations has been involved in attempts to protect civilians. Undermining these protection efforts is the large number of illicitly traded small arms and light weapons in the country. Illicitly traded arms, especially in countries in the grip of war, create serious problems throughout the world, and this is one of many concerns about the arms trade.

The conflict in the Democratic Republic of the Congo has been one of the deadliest wars of its time, with more than 5 million people in this country of approximately 65 million dying between 1998 and 2008.[1] Though the United Nations imposed an arms embargo on the Democratic Republic of the Congo in 2003, the embargo has been violated repeatedly, with weapons reaching the Democratic Republic of the Congo primarily from Uganda and Rwanda. Many weapons that end up in conflict areas around the world, including the Democratic Republic of the Congo, started out as legal weapons.

There is one weapon for every ten people worldwide, and more than half are owned by civilians. It is estimated that there are approximately one-quarter of a billion small arms and light weapons in the United States, more than 100 million in the Middle East, almost a million in both Europe and Latin America, and close to half a million in both North Asia and Sub-Saharan Africa. The United States is the biggest exporter of arms, exporting more than half a billion dollars worth of firearms a year. Italy, Brazil, Germany, Belgium, and

1. Human Rights News, "Democratic Republic of Congo: Q and A." http://hrw.org.

Russia also are key exporters, with each exporting more than $100 million of firearms annually.[2]

In an attempt to address the problem of small arms and light weapons worldwide, the United Nations designated the 9th of July as Small Arms Destruction Day. The United States has joined in the annual observance and, in 2007, reached the milestone of destroying the millionth weapon since the program started in 2001. U.S. projects helping to destroy conventional weapons (not just small arms), as well as efforts to provide physical security and stockpile management of arms and munitions, are under way in Afghanistan, Albania, Angola, Burundi, the Democratic Republic of the Congo, the Republic of the Congo, Guinea-Bissau, Iraq, Lebanon, Montenegro, Uganda, and Ukraine.

2. Mvemba Phezo Dizolele et al., "The Toll of Small Arms," *New York Times*, September 5, 2006.

The Arms Trade in the Middle East Could Lead to a Dangerous Arms Race

Peter Brookes

Peter Brookes is a Heritage Foundation senior fellow and a former deputy assistant secretary of defense who also served in the Navy and with the CIA.

Instability in Iraq, sectarian violence, Islamic extremism, ethnic rivalries, the rise of Iran and questions about America's long-term commitment to the region are making for a Middle East more unsettled than at any time in recent memory.

So it shouldn't come as a shock that a Middle East arms race—both conventional and nuclear—may be in the offing as states hustle to get weapons that ensure their security bets are well hedged against current and future threats.

Instability in the Middle East

Taking a look at the political-military landscape around the Middle East, from the Eastern Mediterranean to the Persian Gulf, there's no shortage of well-founded reasons for strategic insomnia in regional capitals.

Topping the list of problems is the cocky, ascendant Islamic Republic of Iran. In the eyes of many, Tehran's regional policies are more troubling than at any time since the 1979 Iranian revolution and the fall of the Shah.

Although none of the region's Muslim states likes the fact that Israel has long had an undeclared nuclear weapons program, the likelihood that Iran's ayatollahs will become atomic seems all but inevitable. Iran is also supporting elements of

Peter Brookes, "Arms Racing: Middle East Nations Rush to Shore Up Sophisticated Weapons Stocks," *Armed Forces Journal*, vol. 145, November 2007, pp. 8–10. Copyright © 2008 *Armed Forces Journal*. Reproduced by permission.

the insurgencies in Iraq (Shiite militias) and Afghanistan (the Taliban). As if that weren't enough, Tehran is propping up fundamentalist Hezbollah in Lebanon and radical Hamas in the Gaza Strip.

The Islamic Revolutionary Guard Corps' Navy is conducting aggressive maneuvers in the Persian Gulf amid threats by Tehran to attack oil facilities—and close the strategic Strait of Hormuz to tanker traffic.

Syria is giving its neighbors heartburn, as well. Its close ties with predominantly Persian Iran make none of the region's Arab states very happy; nor does Damascus' blind eye to the hordes of jihadists, who transit Syria to destabilize Iraq. The Israeli raid into Syria in September [2007] against a "military target" has everyone chattering—and jittery. The possibility of Syrian-North Korean cooperation on anything beyond ballistic missiles, such as a nuclear program, is utterly unnerving.

Moreover, last summer saw no shortage of rumors of an impending Syrian-Israeli war, or even another Israeli-Hezbollah conflict. The militant Lebanese Shiite group spent the past year re-arming, courtesy of Iranian and Syrian sponsors.

No one in the Middle East, with the possible exception of Iran and Syria, takes comfort in the sectarian and ethnic violence in Iraq, either—or at the idea that Iraq will spin apart into its Shiite, Sunni and Kurdish components.

Middle Eastern states are taking steps to shore up their security.

The rise of militant Islam is another cause of dyspepsia in the region's capitals. Lebanon fought for several months this year against an al-Qaida-inspired (possibly al-Qaida-associated) group, Fatah al Islam, that was holed up in a Palestinian refugee camp.

In a summer stunner, Hamas forcefully expelled its political rival, secular Fatah, from the Gaza Strip, creating concern not only for the Middle East peace process, but also that Gaza might become an operating base for even more regional militancy. It goes without saying that no state is sanguine about the possibility of a yet-to-be identified Taliban-like resistance movement or homegrown al-Qaida-style wannabes popping up in their midst.

Arms Buyers and Sellers in the Middle East

Not surprisingly, as the winds of war swirl across the region, Middle Eastern states are taking steps to shore up their security. As a result, there's no shortage of arms buyers and sellers.

Last summer [2007], the U.S. announced $20 billion in arms sales to Saudi Arabia and neighboring Persian Gulf states: Kuwait, Oman, Bahrain, Qatar and the United Arab Emirates [UAE]. Although the sales are still controversial on Capitol Hill—surprisingly, in some cases, more so than in Israel—the deal reportedly includes Joint Direct Attack Munitions, electronic warfare gear, UAVs [unmanned aerial vehicles], fighter upgrades, missile defense systems and new naval vessels. Another $13 billion in weapons was proposed for Egypt over 10 years. And Israel, ever mindful of maintaining its qualitative military edge, could get as much as $30 billion worth of new U.S. arms and equipment over the same period.

Russia, no shrinking violet when it comes to arms sales, is also increasingly active in the Middle East. Russia is now the world's second biggest arms seller to the developing world—including supplying the lion's share of Iran's conventional arms.

In fact, Russia agreed to sell Iran $700 million worth of surface-to-air missile (SAM) systems (likely the TOR M-1) last year, which would come in handy in defending Iran's nuclear-related sites against air attack. Moscow also plans to upgrade Tehran's Su-24 and MiG-29 aircraft (some famously flown to Iran during the 1991 Persian Gulf War by fleeing Iraqi pilots), and T-72 main battle tanks. Iran is rumored to be interested in S-300 SAMs, Su-30 fighters and Il-78 airborne tankers, too.

Russia has also forgiven most—maybe all—of Syria's Cold War arms debt, allowing Syrian generals to shop till they drop. Although information is murky, Damascus may be into Moscow for $1 billion in air defense systems, possibly the Pantsyr-S1E.

Moscow is playing in Washington's sandbox, too, reaching an agreement with the UAE in September for air defense systems and armored personnel carriers, as well as the launching of the DubaiSat-1 satellite.

The British are in the arms games, as well. Notwithstanding allegations of corruption in an earlier Tornado jet deal, Saudi Arabia (now the developing world's third-largest arms buyer) has agreed to buy 72 Eurofighter Typhoon jets, worth almost $9 billion.

Asians are also increasingly involved in the Middle East arms bazaar. China will have a world-class defense industry in the next 10 to 15 years, and is increasingly interested in getting its foot in the arms market door. Beijing already provides Tehran with a number of systems, including the highly-capable C-802 anti-ship cruise missiles. (Hezbollah, or the Iranian Islamic Revolutionary Guard Corps, used this missile against an Israeli destroyer during the 2006 war.)

In addition, in the late 1980s, China secretly sold Saudi Arabia the nuclear-capable, medium-range DF-3 (CSS-2) ballistic missile. Some analysts believe Beijing is involved in upgrading these 20-year-old missiles for deterring Iran.

North Korea hawks its favorite export, ballistic missiles, in the Middle East, too. Pyongyang has sold its medium-range No Dong technology to the Iranians for their Shahab missile, as well as short-range Scud missiles to the Syrians.

Peddling Arms or Influence?

Some insist the avalanche of prospective weapons deals is part of a Bush administration plan to contain Iran—plus emphasize America's long-term commitment to regional security, especially with rough sledding in—and calls for withdrawal from—Iraq.

According to Secretary of State Condoleezza Rice, the arms sales aim to "bolster forces of moderation and support a broader strategy to counter the negative influences of al-Qaida, Hezbollah, Syria and Iran." The Bush administration may also be trying to encourage Middle Eastern states such as Saudi Arabia and Egypt to assist Iraq, which many Sunni Arab nations see as dominated by the Shiites, symbolized by Prime Minister Nouri al-Maliki. Indeed, the Saudis have snubbed Maliki since he took office, refusing to meet him. Riyadh apparently sees him as a pawn of Tehran—and as not having done enough to protect Iraq's Sunni population. Saudi Arabia still doesn't have an embassy in Baghdad.

Washington may also be trying to ply the likes of Riyadh and Cairo with arms sales to advance the Israeli-Palestinian peace process, rein in Hamas, loosen Damascus' embrace of Tehran and ensure continued access to regional energy supplies. Some gulf nations are eager to have a powerful backer in the face of Iran's growing strength; those that host U.S. forces or bases (40,000 ashore; 20,000 afloat) want the capability to protect themselves from retribution should the Iran matter go "hot."

The situation is, without question, troubling.

Russia wants to increase its clout in the Middle East, through arms sales—or otherwise. During the Cold War, the Soviet Union had a significant amount of clout in the region based on its anti-Israel and anti-American stance. Today, Russian nostalgia for the good old days, as well as its desire to develop markets for its competitive but declining arms industries, guide Kremlin policy—not to mention developing sway with Gulf states for the formation of a natural gas OPEC [Organization of the Petroleum Exporting Countries].

Moscow is also interested in balancing U.S. power (Russian President Putin visited the UAE, Qatar and Saudi Arabia this year[2007]) and discouraging anyone (e.g., Saudi Arabia or Iran) from causing mischief among Russia's restive Muslim population.

British interests generally align themselves with American goals, and China, now the world's second-largest energy consumer, is keen on access to energy supplies, including investing $100 billion in the Iranian energy sector over the next 25 years.

The situation is, without question, troubling, but it gets worse.

There's good reason to expect possible clandestine nuclear weapons research and development programs among the region's newest nuclear aspirants.

The Danger of the Region's Nuclear Programs

Iran is obviously involved in a nuclear program that includes uranium enrichment and the development of the complete nuclear fuel cycle. Many believe it reeks of a clandestine nuclear weapons program, despite Tehran's protestations to the contrary. Although good estimates are hard to come by as a result of a lack of transparency in the Iranian program, estimates of an Iranian nuclear breakout range from three years on one end to a decade or more at the other. Worse yet, Iranian nuclear denial and deception games are inspiring others in the region to get into the atomic act, as well, spurring not only a conventional arms race, but potentially a nuclear one.

Just since last year, as suspicions about Iran have grown to a near fever pitch, several states, including Egypt and Saudi Arabia, told the United Nations' [U.N.] International Atomic Energy Agency they're launching "peaceful" nuclear programs.

Beyond Egypt and Saudi Arabia, Algeria, Morocco, Tunisia, the United Arab Emirates, Turkey, Jordan and Yemen have openly talked of pursuing nuclear power in recent months. And there's no guarantee the list won't grow even longer, either. This is no small undertaking. Building a nuclear program takes six to 10 years and considerable expense ($1 billion-plus per reactor). But eyeing Iran's breakneck pace, regional states may well think they don't have a moment to waste.

In addition, considering the likely militarization of Iran's program, there's good reason to expect possible clandestine nuclear weapons research and development programs among the region's newest nuclear aspirants.

Will we see a map of the Middle East dotted with new peaceful nuclear-power reactors—or dotted with new nuclear-weapons states?

There's little doubt that these states' decisions to start nuclear programs—or restart long-mothballed programs— were guided and tempered at least in part by their plummeting faith in anyone's ability, especially the U.N.'s, to rein in Iran's runaway nuclear program.

One can't ignore motivation that derives from Israel's undeclared nuclear arsenal, either. In fact, calls for a Middle East nuclear-weapons-free zone have been revived, aimed at Israel—and now, of course, Iran.

The question is: In a decade or so, if these programs do go forward, will we see a map of the Middle East dotted with new peaceful nuclear-power reactors—or dotted with new nuclear-weapons states? Or both?

In many respects, security problems in the Middle East only seem to be growing, fueled by ideology, ethnic and sectarian divisions, as well as traditional issues of geopolitics, nationalism, sovereignty and hegemony.

Although Iran's rise is a significant destabilizing factor, it's not the only one. In fact, according to Undersecretary of State Nicholas Burns, "the Iran element is one factor, but it's not the overriding factor why we're doing [the arms sales]."

It is also likely that the Bush administration wants to make an unambiguous investment in regional friends and allies and U.S. strategic interests in the region, while balancing the big power political push of Russia and China for influence, too.

Is a Middle East arms race inevitable? Not necessarily. But in the end, a lot will depend on the unfolding of difficult-to-predict events, especially surrounding Iran—meaning Washington had best be prepared for a wide range of troubling possibilities.

Arms Can End Up in the Hands of Extremists

Christopher Dickey

Christopher Dickey is the Paris bureau chief and Middle East regional editor for Newsweek *magazine. Previously he worked for* The Washington Post *as Cairo bureau chief and Central America bureau chief.*

On the afternoon of Feb. 5, 2006, at a small church in the Turkish Black Sea city of Trabzon, Father Andrea Santoro was kneeling in prayer when a bullet from an Austrian-made Glock 9mm pistol hit him in the back and pierced his heart. The soft-spoken 60-year-old Italian priest, who lived in poverty ministering to the city's tiny Christian community, slumped to the floor, and the killer squeezed off another round. "Allahu akbar!"—"God is great"—said the shooter, a 15-year-old boy with a grudge against the West.

In May of last year, another Muslim fanatic, guns blazing, attacked Turkey's supreme court in Ankara. Four justices were wounded and one was killed. The assassin's weapons of choice were a pair of Glock pistols.

Arms End Up on the Black Market

The attacks were no mystery. What puzzled Turkish police was the weapons' origin. Glocks are high-quality sidearms, but by last year they had practically become common street weapons in Turkey. More than 1,000 had been taken from criminals, guerrillas, terrorists and assassins all over the country, and authorities believed tens of thousands more had found their way onto the black market—but from where? The Austrian government repeatedly checked the serial numbers of the murder weapons. The manufacturer informed Ankara that the pistols were consigned originally to "'US Mission Iraq' [formerly the Coalition Provisional Authority], address: Republican Presidential Compound, Ministry of the Interior, Baghdad, Iraq."

The U.S. military has investigated the problem repeatedly—and the losses look more appalling every time.

There are many more where those came from. At least three U.S. government agencies are now investigating the massive "disappearance" and diversion of weapons Washington intended for Iraqi government forces that instead have spread to militants and organized gangs across the region. The potential size of the traffic is stunning. A report by the U.S. Government Accountability Office last month showed that since 2004, some 190,000 AK-47 assault rifles and pistols, bought with U.S. money for Iraqi security forces, have gone missing.

At retail prices in the United States, a Glock 19 costs about $500. On the black market in Turkey, it can fetch up to $3,500, according to the national police. A senior Turkish security official, speaking on condition of anonymity because of diplomatic sensitivities, said his government estimates some 20,000 U.S.-bought Glock 9mm pistols have been brought from Iraq into his country over the last three years. "The problem on our side is that this corruption is so big they [the Iraqi and U.S. governments] cannot stop it," said the official.

The U.S. military has investigated the problem repeatedly—and the losses look more appalling every time. Major U.S. arms transfers began when Gen. David Petraeus was commander of the Multi-National Security Transition Command—Iraq (MNSTC-I), better known as Minsticky. Its mission was to train, arm and organize Iraq's military and police forces, but the Iraqis' weapons came via the State Department, and the supply line was actually run by private contractors. A certain sense of drama militated against good bookkeeping, too. In a recent radio interview, Petraeus—now the commander of all Coalition forces in Iraq—reminisced about helicopters ferrying weapons to Iraqi troops under fire at night in Najaf. Men were "kicking two battalions' worth of equipment off the ramp and getting out of there while we could," he said.

The Mysterious Death of an Army Ethics Professor

But there were also signs of problems more serious than bad record-keeping. One of Petraeus's subordinates, Col. Theodore Westhusing, had taken leave from his position as a professor of ethics at West Point to serve a six-month tour as commander of the unit training counterterrorism and Special Operations Forces. By the spring of 2005, Westhusing had grown increasingly concerned about the corruption he thought he saw in the program. He was especially upset after receiving an anonymous letter on May 19, 2005, which claimed there was outright fraud by government contractors. Among the alleged problems: failure to account for almost 200 guns.

Westhusing passed the letter up the chain of command. A few days later he wrote a formal memo saying he thought the charges were off-base. But at the same time his conversations and e-mails with his family members became cryptic and he seemed concerned for his safety. Colleagues said he looked exhausted and preoccupied. On June 5, 2005, Westhusing was found dead in his temporary quarters at Camp Dublin near Baghdad airport, apparently having shot himself with his own pistol. "I cannot support a [mission] that leads to corruption, human rights abuses and liars," he wrote in a note found near his body. "Death before being dishonored any more. Trust is essential—I don't know who to trust anymore."

Military investigators concluded that Westhusing's death was a suicide and that the various complaints he leveled against commanders and contractors were "unfounded." Westhusing had had trouble fitting in with other officers, became increasingly withdrawn and seemed depressed when he thought his tour might be extended. But his older brother doesn't believe he killed himself, especially not, as it happened, on his mother's birthday. "Everything he talked about and reported up his chain of command is coming out now: contract fraud, stolen guns and equipment, issues with killings," says Tim Westhusing, who works for IBM in Oklahoma.

General Petraeus declined to comment for the record on the death of Westhusing or the diversion of arms. A senior Pentagon official, talking on background because of the issue's sensitivity, said that a few weeks ago Defense Secretary Robert Gates sent the department's general counsel, Jim Haynes, to "meet with the Turks, hear their concerns and convey that we take them very seriously." The senior official added that in December 2005 the Pentagon launched a "wide-ranging" investigation—which he said was still ongoing—into corruption among contractors in Iraq.

Missing Weapons Are Not Publicly Accounted For

But the first detailed investigation of the missing weapons was conducted last summer by Stuart Bowen, the Special Inspector General for Iraq Reconstruction. His team found there was a special problem with Glocks: 13,180 were missing, worth as much as $46 million on the black market. The more recent GAO study puts the total figure for missing pistols closer to 80,000.

Neither report comes to any conclusion about where those guns went—at least not publicly. A classified version of the GAO report will be submitted to Congress next month [September 2007], and the Pentagon's investigation has been handed over to its criminal division and the FBI. But the Turks know what happened to hundreds of those guns, and the congregation of a little church in Trabzon knows only too well how one of them was used.

Arms Frequently Go to Countries with Poor Human Rights Records

Lerna K. Yanik

Lerna K. Yanik is assistant professor in the department of political science at Bilkent University in Ankara, Turkey.

As the first Gulf War started in January 1991, the Coalition forces that were determined to remove the Iraqi occupation forces in Kuwait quickly discovered that some of their weapons were not quite usable. While the French were unable to use their Mirage fighter jets because the Coalition forces could not distinguish the French Mirages from "enemy" Iraqi Mirages sold to Iraq by France, it also soon became clear that the radar jamming systems purchased by Iraq from the British created a great danger for the Coalition forces. The French and the British were not alone in arming Iraq, a country that was at war with Iran and that brutally repressed its minorities. The Soviet Union, the United States, Germany, and many other countries throughout the 1970s and the 1980s had literally raced with each other to sell arms, both conventional and unconventional, to Iraq. Similarly, before the Rwandan genocide in 1994, various countries, including South Africa, Israel, Albania, France, and Bulgaria, had no problems showering arms on a country where ethnic tensions were on the brink of explosion.

Examples of Arms Transfers to Countries with Poor Human Rights Records

These two examples are the best-known cases of arms sales by mostly Western powers to countries undergoing violations of

Lerna K. Yanik, "Guns and Human Rights: Major Powers, Global Arms Transfers, and Human Rights Violations," *Human Rights Quarterly*, vol. 28, May 2006, pp. 357–360, 388. Copyright © 2006 by The Johns Hopkins University Press. Reproduced by permission.

human rights in conflict. Yet, they are not part of a distant history. While the international community has embargoed the delivery of arms to several countries in conflict, the practice of delivering arms to conflict zones or to countries with imperfect human rights still continues, and there are many examples. For example, in the early 1990s, Italian arms and ammunition made their way to Sierra Leone and Congo, two countries embroiled in ethnic conflict. Similarly, *The Guardian*, in a July 2002 article, noted sharp increases in British arms exports to Israel, Pakistan, Turkey, Saudi Arabia, Indonesia, Jordan, and India. On the other hand, when the approval of arms sales to Nepal, a country in conflict and with a poor human rights record, surfaced in Belgium in July 2002, it led to the resignation of the Finance Minister Magda Alvoet. More importantly, the United States, a country that is considered to have the most sophisticated laws on arms transfers, decided to lift the sanctions imposed on India and Pakistan after 11 September 2001 and resumed the transfer of arms to both of these countries as new allies of the United States in the "War Against Terrorism."

Arms transfers to countries with poor human rights records have opportunity costs in terms of human and international security.

The examples of arms transfers to countries with problematic human rights records are countless. There are many more contextual examples cited in the reports of various advocacy groups, but so far, there has been limited research classifying these flows. . . . Some statistical studies have argued that after the end of the Cold War, the United States started to pay attention to human rights conditions in recipient countries; and thus, [according to researcher Shannon Lindsey Blanton] "countries that abuse human rights were less likely to be recipients of American arms." While these statistical studies tend to classify arms transfers as "less likely," when we look at the practice, most supplier countries, including the United States, eventually uphold their commercial and national security concerns and turn their backs on human rights concerns that they have long championed.

The Possibility of an International Code for Arms Transfers

The relation between arms transfers and the exacerbation of conflicts and human rights violations has long been an established fact. This nasty relation between arms trade and human rights forced supplier countries, which correspond mostly to the most developed countries of the world, to enact various laws and codes at the national and international level. For example, supplier countries enacted laws prohibiting or "discouraging" arms transfers to countries with poor human rights records. Despite all of these laws and codes, supplier countries do transfer conventional weapons to countries with dubious human rights records. This practice, in most cases, eventually creates a cycle that worsens human rights conditions in these recipient countries. . . .

In 2005, the idea of an international arms treaty gained speed one more time. In March 2005, British Foreign Secretary Jack Straw declared his country's intention to establish an international arms treaty within the United Nations. Following this, in October 2005, the Council of the European Union "acknowledged the support, in all parts of the world, for an international treaty to establish common standards for the global trade in conventional arms." The Council also stated that the platform for such a trade should be the United Nations.

Given the competitive nature of the current arms market, it is doubtful that major suppliers would be willing to embrace an international code with real and stringent controls on their arms exports. Furthermore, the US strategy following

11 September 2001, which has been to build "coalitions" at all cost, has resulted in the lifting of sanctions to countries such as India, Pakistan, Azerbaijan, and Tajikistan and the increase of arms transfers to many other countries with dubious human rights records, creates doubts about the intentions of the great powers. These recent developments demonstrate that what the world needs is a change in mentality more than a change in codes. Arms transfers to countries with poor human rights records have opportunity costs in terms of human and international security. Arms in the wrong hands likely worsen human rights conditions and curtail human development by draining precious resources in the recipient country. As the world witnessed during the first Gulf War, in Afghanistan, and elsewhere, weapons can just as well be used against supplier countries.

Small Arms Cause More Damage Worldwide than Weapons of Mass Destruction

Raenette Taljaard

Raenette Taljaard is a member of the South African Parliament, senior lecturer in the School of Public and Development Management at the University of the Witwatersrand, and director of the Helen Suzman Foundation in South Africa.

As the world watched the principal US investigator, David Kay, come up empty-handed in his search for weapons of mass destruction (WMD) in Iraq, coalition force soldiers and civilians continued to perish. They are being killed by small arms and light weapons. Rocket-propelled grenades continue to rock the frontline of the post-conflict reconstruction effort as weapons inspectors keep up the hunt for WMD in Iraq. Meanwhile soldiers uncover small arms and light weapons caches with a near hum-drum regularity in Iraq.

The Focus on WMD Is Misplaced

The real weapons of mass destruction are not the ones being sought by David Kay in Iraq. To millions of people across the world they are the small arms and light weapons that wreak havoc and cause significant loss of life every day. As UN [United Nations] Secretary-General Kofi Annan has said: "The death toll from small arms dwarfs that of all other weapons systems—and in most years greatly exceeds the toll of the atomic bombs that devastated Hiroshima and Nagasaki. In terms of the carnage they cause, small arms, indeed, could be described as 'weapons of mass destruction.' Yet there is still no global non-proliferation regime to limit their spread."

Over 5,000 people died in 1988 in the town of Halabja when the Hussein regime launched a chemical attack on innocent Kurdish Iraqis. This compares with over 300,000 small arms-related deaths per year with incalculable costs for peace and development foregone in some of the most poverty-stricken countries. It is estimated that wars fought with small arms and light weapons in Africa over the past decade have claimed more than 20 million victims. An estimated 2 million children have been killed, 5 million people have been handicapped, 12 million people have been left without shelter, and 17 million have been driven from their homes and/or countries.

With the global security and disarmament community renewing its focus on the proliferation of WMD in the context of the war on terror, and with new threats to global peace and security emanating from North Korea and Iran, there is a grave danger that the global diffusion of small arms and light weapons will slip onto the backburner of disarmament debates and action.

A Huge Global Problem

A recent report by Oxfam and Amnesty International expresses concern that the global campaign against terrorism has made handguns and other small arms more easily available in some countries as suppliers have loosened export controls for states allied to the US in the 'war on terror'. In the same minute in which one person dies from armed violence, 15 new arms are manufactured for sale. There is no doubt that an expansion of the arms caches already in existence today will have dire consequences for developed and developing countries alike.

While WMD is, yet again, taking center-stage, WIDs [weapons of individual destruction] pose an equally grave and great challenge, not only to developing countries gripped in conflict or making their way painstakingly towards demobilization and peace, but to global security. Small arms are tools imminently suitable to exacerbating the phenomenon of failed states. In Africa, small arms also find their way far too easily into the hands of child soldiers, many of whom, orphaned by the ravages of the HIV/AIDS crisis, turn to rebel groups and militias for their livelihood and survival.

A rash of weekly shootings and a recent blast that killed an innocent schoolteacher in eastern Kosovo raised international concern over uncontrolled weapons in this post-conflict zone. With UN estimates putting the number of small arms in Kosovo (ranging from Kalashnikovs to AK47s and rocket propelled grenade launchers) at approximately half a million, the UNDP [United Nations Development Programme] recently launched a three-month public awareness campaign that will be followed by tough criminal penalties for illegal gun ownership. According to UN estimates, Afghanistan is home to between 500,000 and 1.5 million weapons. Estimates show some 300,000 child soldiers around the world are carrying pistols and machine guns. There are at least 639 million firearms in circulation in the world today, with 1,134 companies in 98 countries actively producing these weapons.

WMD proliferation has caused less loss of human life than WID diffusion across our global village.

There can be no doubt that the spread of WIDs in Africa has exacerbated near-intractable inter-state conflicts and civil wars, contributed to human rights violations where the population gets caught in the crossfire, and undermined political and economic development by entrenching conflict economies fuelled by commodities and guns. In sub-Saharan Africa alone it is estimated that 30 million small arms and light weapons are in circulation. Many of these weapons circulate from conflict zone to conflict zone with ruthless arms brokers extracting huge profits. The peddling of small arms and light weapons is deeply embedded in conflict economies—whether civil war-based conflict or conflict intertwined with organized crime syndicates—where natural resources, such as timber, minerals or conflict diamonds or other products such as narcotics are traded for these WIDs. Small arms therefore not only pose a disarmament challenge but also a formidable challenge for development and humanitarian intervention and assistance.

The failure to commit seriously to addressing the proliferation of WID is unconscionable.

The Global Community Must Take Action

Against this stark backdrop of human devastation, the international community cannot afford to pick favorites for disarmament debates when it has such clear proof that WMD proliferation has caused less loss of human life than WID diffusion across our global village. Worse still, it cannot afford to squander what little political will can and must be mustered to tackle the small arms challenge. Already the signals on political will are disconcerting. The UN Security Council's Expert Panel reports on Sierra Leone, Liberia and Angola reveal how contemptuously arms brokers have defied UN arms embargos and show a near complete inaction on the part of the international community to enforce them. In addition the recent UN Conference on small arms failed to enact the new small arms non-proliferation regime called for by Secretary General Annan.

The international community should adopt an all-encompassing new Arms Trade Treaty with clear provisions regulating transfers, marking and tracing of weapons, the role of brokers and containing prohibitions on transfers to non-state actors. Instead, it has failed to rise to the challenge and adopted a mere political agreement—the Programme of Action to Prevent, Combat and Eradicate the Illicit Trade in Small Arms and Light Weapons in All Its Aspects. While the programme of action calls on states to undertake a host of steps at a national, regional and multilateral level, these steps are not binding or compulsory. States can proceed in a discretionary fashion at any pace, if at all.

The failure to commit seriously to addressing the proliferation of WID is unconscionable. The international community must realize the link between small arms and new security threats, and act swiftly to tighten regulatory mechanisms to counteract their proliferation. There can be no more lost opportunities or neglect of WID in favor of WMD disarmament issues. In the post Cold War security threat world, both WMD and WID must be seen—against the backdrop of failed states—as indispensable parts of a disarmament continuum. This means that key countries, such as the United States, must be willing to engage the crucial questions of the need to establish and maintain controls over private ownership of these deadly weapons and their proliferation to non-state groups. This will require Washington to work hand-in-hand with the international community on disarmament matters.

Investing in the Arms Trade Involves an Ethical Dilemma

Alicia Wyllie

Alicia Wyllie is a journalist who writes about financial issues.

There is something distasteful about companies that sell weapons for profit: companies that don't merely produce enough arms to protect their own homelands, but actively sell them to other, possibly less scrupulous countries, to raise enough cash to pay fat-cat salaries to directors and bumper dividends to shareholders.

Many Invest in Weapons Without Knowing It

Millions of people have been killed in wars since 1945, 90 per cent of whom, according to the Campaign Against Arms Trade (CAAT), were non-combatants, and at least half were children. And yet, despite these statistics, the majority of us are not only happy to stomach the companies that make the weapons being listed on the Stock Exchange (which implies their main aim is mammon [money] not morality), but are also happy to invest in them.

Most of us are indirect investors though the pension funds, endowment policies and Individual Savings Accounts into which we diligently pay every month. We are, none the less, investing in other people's misery. There is only a small minority of us who have had the courage of our own convictions and have invested in one of the many ethical funds available.

For those who haven't, the good news is that defence companies have been one of the few areas of the stock market,

Alicia Wyllie, "Buying into the Arms Trade: Defence Budgets Are Rising, but Should We Invest in the Companies That Benefit?" *New Statesman*, July 8, 2002, p. xxvi. Copyright © 2002 New Statesman, Ltd. Reproduced by permission.

along with the controversial sectors of tobacco and beverages, that have been protecting the value of our retirement funds.

Increased Defence Spending Improves Stock Performance

This year, defence stocks, such as BAE Systems and Smiths Industries, have jumped 20 per cent in value, behind tobacco, which tops the performance table with a 40 per cent increase, but ahead of beverages with a 13 per cent increase.

The strong performance posted by the defence sector is hardly surprising, given the "positive" environment in which it now finds itself. The events of 11 September, and the reaction of the US, have meant that defence companies are now thriving.

President [George W.] Bush has now proposed to increase defence spending by $48bn in 2003. That is $38bn over the increase needed to keep pace with inflation. He also plans to double the recently announced spending on homeland defence to $38bn—it was close to zero before 11 September. Taken together, the total increase of approximately $86bn is equal to around 0.7 per cent of the GDP [Gross Domestic Product] projected for 2003. As the US Center for Economic and Policy Research acidly points out, this amount is almost precisely equal to America's 75-year shortfall in social security.

The UK, too, is planning to increase its defence budget, from nearly £23bn in 2000/2001 to almost £25bn in 2003/2004. That is, the MoD [Ministry of Defence] says, the first sustained above-inflation increase in defence spending since the mid-1980s.

Then there is the renewed enthusiasm for America's national missile defence programme, aka "son of star wars", seen since 11 September.

A Dilemma for Investors

This increased momentum in arms building means that the peace dividend, which was supposed to materialise after the cold war ended, has never truly been realised. But does this mean that the people who manage our money will continue investing in defence companies? Not necessarily. History has shown that war has a limited effect on the share prices of defence companies—though that evidence is relevant only if the war against terrorism eventually does end.

In addition, many defence companies also have commercial interests. This means that war can, in fact, have a negative effect on their returns. BAE Systems, for example, has a 20 per cent stake in Airbus. These commercial aerospace activities were obviously badly affected by the downturn in air travel after 11 September.

There is a fine line to tread between money and morals.

However, except for the US, it is doubtful whether major increases in defence spending could get past the electorates in most western countries. The UK may be about to witness the first above-inflation increase since the mid-1980s, but we are still a long way from 1984, when defence spending accounted for 5.3 per cent of GDP. Today, the figure is down to 2.5 per cent.

Whether you are a pure pacifist or just believe that arms should only be used for defence purposes, it is the sale of weapons to conflict-ridden countries such as India that should make us question our priorities. Can we trust defence companies to do the right thing when they have a profit motive, any more than we could trust Railtrack to maintain the UK's rail infrastructure?

Probably not. But then, if they help boost the value of our pension funds, perhaps we don't really have anything to complain about. There is a fine line to tread between money and morals for both companies and consumers.

The Arms Trade May Involve Corporate Welfare

Charles M. Sennott

Charles M. Sennott, former foreign correspondent for The Boston Globe, *is executive editor, co-founder, and vice president of Global News Enterprises, a web-based news service.*

After Lockheed Martin clinched one of its largest deals ever in Europe, Prime Minister Leszek Miller of Poland was taken for a spin last week [January 9, 2003] in the same kind of F-16 fighter jet that his country is purchasing. He watched from the cockpit while a second F-16 performed rolls and tactical maneuvers for his benefit.

Consider this private air show a kind of customer perk, which the Pentagon confirmed was paid for by the US government at the end of a long marketing campaign by Lockheed. The US government also provided a $3.8 billion loan to Poland, on very favorable terms, to finance the purchase of 48 F-16s, which are manufactured in President [George W.] Bush's home state of Texas.

When they meet at the White House today, Miller and Bush are sure to toast this huge deal. For Poland, the purchase is a matter of national pride, reflecting the country's recent military transformation as a new member of NATO [North Atlantic Treaty Organization]. The deal highlights Bush's personal involvement in pushing for arms deals in which former East Bloc countries switch to American weapons systems.

Critics Say U.S. Government Involved in Corporate Welfare

But arms-industry watchdog groups say the cost of the private air show is just one example of the kind of corporate welfare that goes into these massive and complex business deals. These critics contend the prime minister's test flight raises the question of who is taking whom for a ride in such a massive arms deal.

In a shrinking and fiercely competitive arms industry in Europe, Lockheed's victory has sparked the ire of European economic ministers.

"The Poland arms deal is corporate welfare at its finest," said Ivan Eland, a military analyst at the Cato Institute, a Washington-based, free-market policy group. "The companies are private enterprises, but they are in effect wards of the state when the US government supports and underwrites the deals.

"There are all sorts of hidden subsidies that the US government gives to arms manufacturers, and the Polish prime minister's flight would be just one of them," he said.

Jose Ibarra, a Pentagon spokesman, confirmed that the US government paid for the F-16s to be sent to Poland for the prime minister's flight. "If the US government deems it in our national interest, we pay for it," he said.

Ibarra did not know the cost to taxpayers, but said, "It ain't cheap, that's for sure." Having Air Force pilots take two fighter jets from the US airbase in Aviano, Italy, to Poland could run as high as hundreds of thousands of dollars, one US official estimated.

Washington's support helped Lockheed beat out the French Dassault Aviation offer of Mirage jets, as well as a Swedish-British consortium's offer of Grippen fighter jets, in what industry analysts say is the largest deal for a US arms manufacturer ever in Eastern Europe. The decision was announced Dec. 28 with little fanfare, and approval for the loan sailed through Congress.

Competition for Arms Customers Is Fierce

In a shrinking and fiercely competitive arms industry in Europe, Lockheed's victory has sparked the ire of European economic ministers, especially the French. European critics have accused Poland of betraying their neighbors just after they were invited into the European Union. Some critics in Poland questioned the need for such weapons at all.

At the North Atlantic Treaty Organization summit here in November, the industry battle for the Polish deal was under way behind the scenes. The summit brought seven new Eastern European and Baltic states into NATO and effectively redrew the military map of Europe, bringing the military alliance forged in the Cold War to the borders of Russia. Poland joined NATO in an earlier expansion, in 1998.

Bruce Jackson, director of a bipartisan, nonprofit advocacy group called the US Committee on NATO, had worked for at least six years for the enlargement of NATO and was in Prague celebrating the fruits of that hard work. For Jackson, who recently retired as vice president of Lockheed Martin, the expansion of NATO was more than just a dream of "uniting Europe whole and free," as he put it. It was also helping to create a new market for the US arms manufacturer that had employed him.

And there may be more deals to be had among the new members of NATO admitted at the Prague summit. The Czech Republic, Romania, and other Eastern European and Baltic countries are now being courted by US arms manufacturers to upgrade their military capacity to be NATO "interoperable." That means buying Western hardware to replace older equipment that countries of the former Soviet bloc used in the days of the Warsaw Pact. The transition to NATO often means buying American.

Jackson's advocacy work in the expansion of NATO and Lockheed's arms deal with Poland highlight the political and corporate linkages that make the NATO expansion both a matter of strategic significance for the United States and economic advantage for its arms manufacturers.

US taxpayers often end up subsidizing these sales, while arms manufacturers walk away with huge profits.

Jackson scoffed at critics' complaints that his political passions have anything to do with his former employer's interests. He said he believes that a stronger, bigger NATO means greater security for the United States. Officials from NATO, Poland, and Lockheed all said he carefully avoided lobbying for the company on the F-16 sale.

Arms Deals Involve Questionable Government Subsidy

But William Hartung, a senior research fellow at the World Policy Institute who has researched the costs of NATO expansion to taxpayers, said, "Arms manufacturers like Lockheed are looking to Eastern Europe as the last frontier to squeeze out big fighter jet deals, and they are looking to the US government to pick up the tab."

Industry watchdogs like Eland and Hartung said the Polish arms deal shows how US taxpayers often end up subsidizing these sales, while arms manufacturers walk away with huge profits.

Richard Kirkland, Lockheed's vice president for corporate international business development, said that while the enlargement of NATO did present an important new market, it was a relatively modest one, compared to regions such as the Middle East and Asia.

The Polish sale was supported by the US government through the Pentagon's Foreign Military Financing fund, or FMF, Pentagon officials said. Poland will not have to make payments for eight years and will have at least 15 years to pay back the money at a level of interest which US government officials said they are not allowed to disclose.

The deals are structured around what are known as offset agreements, business arrangements that bring everything from production jobs to technology transfers to the purchasing country as an inducement. In the Polish arms deal, the offset agreements are said to be worth $6 billion to $9 billion.

Labor unions said the offsets encourage the export of jobs overseas. In the Polish deal, for example, the contract to build the F-16 engines was awarded to Pratt & Whitney of Connecticut, which US officials confirmed has agreed to assemble the engines in Poland.

To Hartung, Jackson embodies the link between politics and the arms industry on the road to enlarging NATO.

"You would like to think that the people deciding whether this [NATO expansion] is a good idea for the country would not be being led around by a person like Jackson, whose company has such a great financial interest in the expansion of NATO," Hartung said.

Jackson answered: "The yellow journalism approach of trying to link American internationalists to venal financial motives is all rather depressing. . . . I believe that democracy is worth defending. The Poles made the right decision, which will make the [NATO] alliance stronger and share the responsibilities of collective defense more equitably between the US and our European allies."

Lockheed officials and Jackson himself say he was never a registered lobbyist on behalf of Lockheed. Lockheed also said that it never gave money to the US Committee on NATO, which Jackson helped found. And US and Polish officials said that Jackson, 50, was always careful about avoiding conflicts of interest in his dual roles.

Becoming an Arms Dealer Is Too Easy

Mark Thomas

Mark Thomas is a comedian and reporter in England.

A few months ago I watched a 16-year-old schoolgirl, Ellie, from Oxford, phone a tank manufacturer in Romania. Ellie was part of a group of British students who formed their own arms company and ran it once a week at lunchtime.

"I want to chat to someone about a tank," she said. "What kind of tank?" asked an uncertain eastern European voice.

"A TR-85 M1."

"You want a price?"

"Yes, that would be great."

A month later and Ellie's arms company was quoted a guide price of [£]2.5m for the tank (CD players and cup holders are extra).

Students Set Up an Arms Company

The students attend Lord Williams's Upper School, in Thame, Oxfordshire, and are part of the school's Amnesty International group. Together with a teacher, George Lear, they set up an arms company, Williams Defence—completely legally— from their school premises, as part of a project for Channel 4's *Dispatches* programme.

The *Daily Mail* might be tempted to scream, "Kids taught arms dealing at school" (something it might actually approve of, if the subject were referred to as business studies). In reality, however, the pupils approached the project by discussing the human-rights implications of the UK government's arms licensing policy. They interviewed arms dealers, quizzed politicians and discussed citizenship. They ended up presenting their findings to MPs [members of Parliament] from the quadripartite committee (the select committee with oversight of arms licensing) and the minister responsible, Malcolm Wicks. Parliament, you may remember, is keen that citizenship be taught in schools. I can think of no finer act of citizenship than school students exposing the UK government's failures to control the arms trade.

It was so easy for the students to run an arms company from school.

The students focused on brokerage, which is basically acting as a middleman. For example, someone in the UK could broker AK-47s direct from China to Chad and the guns would not touch British soil. No government controls would have applied before 2004. Since then, laws have been introduced requiring brokers to license such deals. However, the school's investigation highlighted a number of loopholes, particularly for what is called "police and security equipment". The pupils started by locating arms companies on the internet and e-mailing them. It didn't take long to find equipment intended for torture or ill-treatment. They then purchased and shipped it all, legally.

Thumb cuffs sound medieval and, indeed, they are. The internal edges are serrated and will tear flesh quite easily. They are used in China against Tibetan monks, priced $3.65 from Taiwan. Wall cuffs are a single handcuff with a bolt and chain for shackling a prisoner to the wall. These are used all over the world. Straight out of Poland: yours for £9 a set. A sting stick is a long metal baton with spikes and barbs along its shaft. Priced $7.50, it has been used in Tibet and Nepal. The sting stick was brokered to a human-rights activist in the US and then imported into Blighty. The police told me during our filming that if I carried the stick in public I could be arrested for possessing an offensive weapon. Yet there is no UK law to prevent it being brokered around the world.

There is Little Regulation for Arms Dealers

None of these items requires a licence and there is not even a register of arms dealers and brokers. That is why it was so easy for the students to run an arms company from school. Yet it wouldn't be hard to update the lists for torture equipment, and even the Defence Manufacturers Association (the arms trade body) supports a register for arms dealers and brokers.

The students went one step further. Brokering small arms (pistols to AK-47s) needs licences if done from Britain, but if a British citizen steps over the border from Northern Ireland into Ireland they do not. Which is what Williams Defence did, setting up an office at the side of a road and using their mobile phones. They were given quotes for grenade launchers from Pakistan to be sent to Syria ($421), MP5 sub-machine guns to go from Turkey to Mali ([£]750) and pump-action shotguns to go from South Africa to Israeli settlers in Hebron. The dealer in South Africa said he couldn't get a licence to get the guns to Israel but he could send them to a firm in Switzerland or Greece which would do the deal from there.

The *Dispatches* programme shows the need for Europe-wide brokerage controls. In a parallel in Ireland, where no brokerage laws exist, six schoolgirls and a nun brokered electro-shock batons. They were also asked to become agents for Korean electro-shock equipment dealers.

The rule of extraterritoriality should ensure that British law applies to British citizens even when outside the UK. It is used to catch paedophiles. It should be used to prevent British citizens dealing in leg-irons, wherever they are. If we have a law covering long-range missiles, why not one for the real weapons of mass destruction, small arms? Half a million deaths a year are caused by small arms—almost one a minute.

The government ordered a review of arms export laws, to report in 2007. It could do worse than ask the students at Lord Williams's Upper School where UK policy is going wrong.

Organizations to Contact

The editors have compiled the following list of organizations concerned with the issues debated in this book. The descriptions are derived from materials provided by the organizations. All have publications or information available for interested readers. The list was compiled on the date of publication of the present volume; the information provided here may change. Readers need to remember that many organizations take several weeks or longer to respond to inquiries.

Amnesty International
5 Penn Plaza, 16th Floor, New York, NY   10001
(212) 807-8400 • fax: (212) 463-9193
e-mail: admin-us@aiusa.org
Web site: www.amnesty.org

Amnesty International is a worldwide movement of people who campaign for internationally recognized human rights for all. Amnesty International joined with Oxfam International and the International Action Network on Small Arms to set up the Control Arms campaign for an international, legally binding arms trade treaty. Among the many jointly sponsored publications by Amnesty International and others is the briefing paper, "The G8: Global Arms Exporters."

Arms Trade Resource Center
The Arms and Security Project, New York, NY   10013
(212) 431-5808 • fax: (646) 613-1443
e-mail: hartung@newamerica.net
Web site: www.worldpolicy.org/projects/arms/

The Arms Trade Resource Center is a project of the World Policy Institue that was established in 1993 to engage in public education and policy advocacy aimed at promoting restraint in the international arms trade. The Center performs research on the U.S. weapons trade and U.S. arms sales policy, and it publishes reports, magazine articles, and op-ed pieces on the issue, all of which can be found on its Web site.

Council for a Livable World (CLW)

322 4th St. NE, Washington, DC   20002
(202) 543-4100
Web site: www.clw.org

The Council for a Livable World advocates for deep reductions and the eventual elimination of nuclear, chemical, and biological weapons. CLW provides senators and members of Congress with sophisticated technical and scientific information that helps them make intelligent decisions about weapons of mass destruction—nuclear, chemical, and biological weapons—nuclear nonproliferation, and other national security issues. Available at its Web site are numerous policy statements and research reports on weapons in Iran, Iraq, and North Korea, as well as reports on other issues such as the U.S. national missile defense system.

Human Rights Watch (HRW)

350 Fifth Ave, 34th Floor, New York, NY   10118-3299
(212) 290-4700 • fax: (212) 736-1300
e-mail: hrwnyc@hrw.org
Web site: www.hrw.org

Human Rights Watch is dedicated to protecting the human rights of people around the world. HRW investigates human rights abuses, educates the public, and works to change policy and practice. Among its numerous publications is the briefing, "User State Responsibility for Cluster Munition Clearance."

International Action Network on Small Arms (IANSA)

Development House, 56-64 Leonard St., London   EC2A 4LT
   United Kingdom
+44 207 065 0870 • fax: +44 207 065 0871
e-mail: contact@iansa.org
Web site: www.iansa.org

The International Action Network on Small Arms is a global movement that works to stop the proliferation and misuse of small arms and light weapons. IANSA joined with Amnesty International and Oxfam International to set up the Control Arms campaign for an international, legally binding arms trade treaty. Among the many jointly sponsored publications by IANSA and others is the paper, "Guns and Policing: Standards to Prevent Misuse."

Nonviolence International
4000 Albemarle St. #500 NW, Washington, DC   20016
(202) 244-0951 • fax: (202) 244-6396
e-mail: info@nonviolenceinternational.net
Web site: www.nonviolenceinternational.net

Nonviolence International promotes nonviolent action and seeks to reduce the use of violence worldwide. Nonviolence International sponsors events, round tables, and meetings to prevent civil conflict and to promote peace in locations such as the Chechen Republic. The organization has nonviolence training materials available at its Web site.

Oxfam International
226 Causeway St., 5th Floor, Boston, MA   02114-2206
(800) 77-OXFAM • fax: (617) 728-2594
e-mail: info@oxfamamerica.org
Web site: www.oxfam.org

Oxfam is a confederation of organizations working to end poverty and injustice. Oxfam International joined with Amnesty International and the International Action Network on Small Arms to set up the Control Arms campaign for an international, legally binding arms trade treaty. Among the many jointly sponsored publications by Oxfam International and others is the report, "Guns or Growth? Assessing the Impact of Arms Sales on Sustainable Development."

Saferworld
28 Charles Square, London   N1 6HT
   United Kingdom
+44 207 324 4646 • fax: +44 207 324 4647
e-mail: general@saferworld.org.uk
Web site: www.saferworld.org.uk

Saferworld works to create safer communities in places affected by violent crime, conflict, and the impact of small arms and light weapons. Saferworld engages in policy research, technical support to governments, and advocacy to control the spread of small arms and to reduce irresponsible arms exports. Among the many publications available through its Web site is the report, "Good Conduct? Ten Years of the EU Code of Conduct on Arms Exports."

Stockholm International Peace Research Institute (SIPRI)
Signalistgatan 9, Solna   SE-169 70
   Sweden
+46-8-655 97 00 • fax: +46-8-655 97 33
e-mail: sipri@sipri.org
Web site: www.sipri.org

The Stockholm International Peace Research Institute works to contribute to an understanding of the conditions for peaceful solutions of international conflicts and for a stable peace. The institute conducts research on questions of conflict and cooperation of importance for international peace and security. SIPRI publishes numerous reports and policy papers, including *SIPRI Yearbook 2008: Armaments, Disarmament and International Security*.

Bibliography

Books

Richard Bingley   *The Arms Trade.* Chicago, IL: Raintree, 2003.

R. Kim Cragin and Bruce Hoffman   *Arms Trafficking and Colombia.* Santa Monica, CA: RAND National Defense Research Institute, 2003.

Wendy Cukier and Victor W. Sidel   *The Global Gun Epidemic: From Saturday Night Specials to AK-47s.* Westport, CT: Praeger Security International, 2005.

Jeffrey M. Elliot   *The Arms Control, Disarmament, and Military Security Dictionary.* San Bernardino, CA: Borgo Press, 2007.

Douglas Farah and Stephen Braun   *Merchant of Death: Money, Guns, Planes, and the Man Who Makes War Possible.* Hoboken, NJ: Wiley, 2007.

Clive Gifford   *The Arms Trade.* North Mankato, MN: Chrysalis Education, 2004.

Jonathan A. Grant   *Rulers, Guns, and Money: The Global Arms Trade in the Age of Imperialism.* Cambridge, MA: Harvard University Press, 2007.

Michael A. Levi and Michael E. O'Hanlon   *The Future of Arms Control.* Washington, DC: Brookings Institution Press, 2005.

Paul Levine and Ron Smith — *Arms Trade, Security, and Conflict.* New York: Routledge, 2003.

Moises Naim — *Illicit: How Smugglers, Traffickers, and Copycats Are Hijacking the Global Economy.* New York: Anchor Books, 2006.

Joe Roeber — *The Hidden Market: Corruption in the International Arms Trade.* New York: New Press, 2004.

Matthew Schroeder, Rachel Stohl, and Dan Smith — *The Small Arms Trade: A Beginner's Guide.* Oxford: Oneworld Publications, 2007.

Waheguru Pal Singh Sidhu and Ramesh Thaku, eds. — *Arms Control After Iraq: Normative and Operational Challenges.* New York: United Nations University Press, 2006.

Stockholm International Peace Research Institute — *SIPRI Yearbook 2008: Armaments, Disarmament, and International Security.* New York: Oxford University Press, 2008.

Marika Vicziany — *Controlling Arms and Terror in the Asia Pacific: After Bali and Baghdad.* Northampton, MA: Edward Elgar, 2007.

Zeray Yihdego — *The Arms Trade and International Law.* Portland, OR: Hart Publishing, 2007.

Periodicals

Bruce Anderson — "There Are Good Reasons for Selling Arms to China, but Better Ones for Not Doing So," *Spectator*, February 5, 2005.

Frida Berrigan and William D. Hartung — "U.S. Weapons at War 2005: Promoting Freedom or Fueling Conflict?" World Policy Institute, June 2005. www.worldpolicy.org.

Peter Brookes — "The Lifting of the EU Arms Embargo on China: An American Perspective," Heritage Foundation, March 2, 2005. www.heritage.org.

Alan Cullison and Jose de Cordoba — "Russia Reaches Out to Venezuela," *Wall Street Journal*, August 1, 2006.

Clare da Silva — "The Case for an Arms Trade Treaty," *Guardian*, March 10, 2008. www.guardian.co.uk.

Ivan Eland — "What to Do About Pakistan," Antiwar.com, February 4, 2008.

Andrew Feinstein — "Ethical Arms Trade?" *New Statesman*, May 19, 2008.

John Gee — "A Year After Lifting Ban on U.S. Arms Sales, Bush Visits Indonesia," *Washington Report on Middle East Affairs*, January–February 2007.

Andrew Gilligan "Selling Out to China: Andrew Gilligan on Britain's Financial Motives for Breaking with Washington and Lifting the Arms Embargo on Beijing," *Spectator*, February 26, 2005.

Matthew Godsey and Gary Milhollin "A Shell Game in the Arms Race," *The New York Times*, February 25, 2005.

Lindsey Hilsum "China's Economic Interests Are Blooming into Military Ties: Arming Militaries in Latin America, for Example," *New Statesman*, May 15, 2006.

Grace Jean "United States and Britain at Odds over Weapons Sales Regulations," *National Defense*, December 2007.

Fred Kaplan "The Wings of a Hawk: Why Is Bush Selling F-16s to Pakistan?" *Slate*, March 30, 2005. www.slate.com.

David B. Kopel "The U.N. Wants Your Gun," *Wall Street Journal*, July 8, 2006.

Joshua Kurlantzick "A Call to Arms," *Time International (Asia)*, September 24, 2007.

John Larkin and Donald Macintyre "Arsenal of the Axis," *Time International (Asia)*, July 14, 2003.

Rhona MacDonald "Where Next for Arms Control?" *The Lancet*, August 26, 2006.

Helen Mirren "Say No to Murder Inc.," *Globe & Mail*, October 10, 2003.

Daniel Pepper   "Chasing Darfur's Guns," *Mother Jones*, March–April 2008.

Sacramento Bee   "More Arms Increase Risks in Mideast Tinderbox: Bush Administration's Plan for Arms Sales Can Only Increase Dangers in the Region," August 2, 2007.

David E. Sanger   "The World: When Laws Don't Apply; Cracking Down on the Terror-Arms Trade," *New York Times*, June 15, 2003.

Claire Schaeffer-Duffy   "Iraq Allowed to Rearm: Critics Say Embargo Lift May Worsen Iraq's Security Problems," *National Catholic Reporter*, September 10, 2004.

David Shambaugh   "Don't Lift the Arms Embargo on China," *International Herald Tribune*, February 23, 2005.

Thom Shanker   "U.S. Leads Arms Sales to Developing Countries," *International Herald Tribune*, September 30, 2007.

Baker Spring   "A Step Forward in Reforming the U.S. Arms Export Control Process," Heritage Foundation, April 9, 2007. www.heritage.org.

Scott Stedjan   "Arms Trade Treaty: Let the U.S. Opt Out for Now," Foreign Policy in Focus, November 29, 2006. www.fpif.org.

Mark Tran

"A Shot in the Dark: The National Rifle Association is Enraged by a UN Bid to Halt the Spread of Guns," *The Guardian*, June 27, 2006.

Susan Waltz

"U.S. Small Arms Policy: Having It Both Ways," *World Policy Journal*, Summer 2007.

Stephen Zunes

"Arms Transfers to Pakistan Undermine U.S. Foreign Policy Goals," *National Catholic Reporter*, May 20, 2005.

Index

DATE DUE

DEMCO 38-296